UNDERSTANDING MUSIC

Judy Tatchell

Designed by Russell Punter and Mike Ellis
Cover design by Russell Punter

Contents

Illustrated by Ann Johns, Guy Smith, Joe McEwan, Serge Peynet, Roy Barnes

Music consultants: Angela D'Silva, Virginia Rushton, Dave Gelly, David Cunningham, Nick Haines and Cyril Mapstone.

LISTENING TO MUSIC

You do not need to know anything at all about a piece of music in order to enjoy it. However, you may find you enjoy it even more if you know a bit about why it was composed and how it achieves its effect. This book explains how and why different sorts of music developed and why people like them. Once you know what to listen for, you may even find you enjoy types of music that previously did not interest you.

Musical ingredients

Music has certain ingredients, as described on this page. What the music sounds like depends on which ingredients are used and how they are combined. For instance, you could probably identify a piece of 1950s rock and roll because of the type of rhythm, the instruments used and the style of singing.

Beat or pulse

If you clap along to a piece of music, you usually find yourself clapping on the beat or pulse.

Rhythm

Rhythm is a pattern of long and short sounds and pauses which fit round the beat.

Some music, such as drumming, is made up of rhythm alone.

Melody

The melody or tune is the part which you might whistle or sing. It is made up of notes of different pitches. (Pitch describes how high or low a musical note is.) The notes in a tune also have a rhythm.

Structure

Without a structure, music would sound disorganized. Most structures are based on repetition and variation of a theme or tune.

Harmony

Notes which sound good together are said to be in harmony. A lot of music has harmonies added to the melody to make it sound more interesting or to create a particular effect.

The lead singer sings the tune. The backing group sing harmonies.

Tone colour

Each instrument has its own special sound, or tone. The instruments chosen for a piece of music give it a certain sound quality called *timbre* or tone colour.

The choice of instruments is called instrumentation.

Expression

Music played without energy and feeling sounds dead. A musician needs to express the mood of the music, using contrasts in volume, emphasis and so on.

Types of music

You are probably familiar with names for different sorts of music, such as rock, classical or jazz. These names, though, can mean different things to different people, or change their meaning as time goes by.

Most music falls either into the popular or classical group. Here is an explanation of some of the different types of music within these groups.

Popular music

Popular music is what most people play or listen to for entertainment. It tends to rely on a catchy melody and a strong rhythm.

Folk

Folk music is the traditional popular music of a country. It is not usually written down but people pick it up from each other. In some places, folk is still the music that most people sing and dance to. Elsewhere, other forms of popular music have replaced folk.

Jazz

Jazz originated in the early 20th century. There are now several types of jazz. Some are easy to listen to. Others are complicated although many people find these the most exciting. A lot of jazz is improvised (made up on the spot) so each musician brings different ideas to a piece.

Pop and rock

Rock is young people's fashion music. Styles change quickly.

Pop is short for popular music but it usually only means the styles you can hear in the Top 40. The word pop sounds rather trivial, so some people call it rock music or use the names of the different styles, such as soul or rap.

Classical music

Most people use the general term classical music for serious or formal music, mostly written in the past. This sort of music is usually performed in front of a seated, silent audience who do not take part.

The origins of classical music lie in religious music and music written to entertain aristocrats and wealthy people. In fact, a lot of classical music was once the popular music of the upper classes.

Strictly speaking, the term "classical" only applies to European music of the second half of the 18th century. In this book, music from this period is called Classical music, with a capital C.

Styles of classical music from other periods have their own names, such as baroque, Romantic or Nationalist music. All these styles are described later in the book.

Most classical music is written down. You can find out about reading music on pages 18-19.

> Most people enjoy pieces of music from different categories. It is unlikely that you can enjoy all the music in one category and none from another.

ROCK AND POP MUSIC

Rock and pop music is more than just music to listen or dance to. It both sets and reflects current lifestyles and trends.

The birth of rock

Before the 1950s, teenagers did not have their own separate culture and music. Then came two important developments.

1 The 45 rpm record was invented. This gave better sound quality and was less fragile than the old 78 rpm records.

Rpm (revolutions per minute) refers to how fast the record spins round. Until about 1964, record stations liked single records to last for under three minutes.

2 After World War II there was a time of prosperity in the USA. Teenagers had money to spend.

Teenagers became a market worth exploiting so the music industry began to provide them with the music they wanted. This has resulted in an explosion of pop and rock styles since the 1950s. You can read about some of these on pages 5-6.

The number of records sold by Boy George's group Culture Club in 1982 exceeded the total UK pop record sales in 1962. Today, there are about 120 new singles released per week in the UK.

Rock roots

Most styles of pop music are developments and mixtures of past styles. These past styles themselves have their roots in music that pre-dates pop and rock. African music has had the greatest influence on popular music styles, as shown below. The puzzle pieces on the right show some of the other roots of rock and pop.

Here are some of the styles in which African music has had the strongest influence.

Blues

Gospel

Jazz (see page 10).

Calypso (Trinidad).

Mento (Jamaica). Reggae developed from mento.

Salsa (Latin America).

West African speech rhythms survive in rap and house music (see page 6).

Some features of pop performances, such as their informality, have derived from minstrel styles (see page 16).

European folk music

Pop music has borrowed folk instruments, such as the guitar, bagpipes and accordion.

Western classical music

The scales* and harmonies on which a lot of pop music is based came into use in 18th century classical music.

Some songs use orchestral instruments as a backing to add a certain tone colour.

Some groups in the 1960s gave their songs an exotic quality by using Indian instruments.

Indian music

*You can find out what a scale is on page 19.

Rock styles

Rock music changes all the time, as each new generation of musicians reacts to a changing world. The next two pages describe some of the many styles. The examples are all single songs unless otherwise stated.

The most successful musicians take elements from different areas of pop music's past and present and come up with their own mix. Many of the best musicians don't fit any one category, which is why they may not be mentioned here.

The blues
The blues* is black American music. Many of the songs are sad ("blue"). The tunes are based on a set of notes called a blues scale. White music has borrowed blues elements ever since the 50s.

Bessie Smith *Nobody Knows You When You're Down and Out* (1929). John Lee Hooker *Ground Hog* (1950). Album: BB King *My Kind of Blues* (1960).

Gospel music
The first gospel songs were the spirituals* of African slaves converted to Christianity. The joyful, emotional style which developed from these thrives in churches in southern USA.

The Dixie Hummingbirds *Ezekiel Saw the Wheel* (1947). The Staples Singers *We Shall Overcome* (1965). Aretha Franklin *Respect* (1967).

Rhythm and blues
Black workers moving to cities from farms in southern USA took the blues with them. During the 50s, the mixture of blues and gospel, amplified and accompanied by electric guitars, became known as rhythm and blues, or R and B.

Bo Diddley *Who Do You Love* (1956). Chuck Berry *Memphis Tennessee* (1959). Isley Brothers *Twist and Shout* (1962).

Country and western
This was the music of poor white Americans in the 1930s and 40s. It is still the most popular music in southern USA. It remained mostly separate from the influence of black music.

Hank Williams *Take These Chains from My Heart and Set Me Free* (1953). Tammy Wynette *Almost Persuaded, D.I.V.O.R.C.E.* (1968).

Rock and roll
During the mid-50s, white teenagers discovered R and B. White radio stations would not play black music, though. Elvis Presley provided a commercial breakthrough with his mix of R and B and country music. This was rock and roll.

Bill Haley and His Comets *Rock Around the Clock* (1955). Elvis Presley *Blue Suede Shoes* (1956). Jerry Lee Lewis *Great Balls of Fire* (1957). Eddie Cochran *Summertime Blues* (1958).

Soul
Soul is a mixture of gospel and R and B. During the 60s and 70s, though, soul was used as a name for almost any black music. Some styles are named after the record label associated with the sound (such as Motown, Philadelphia or Stax) or they may be given other names, such as funk or disco.

Diana Ross and the Supremes *Where Did Our Love Go* (1964). Marvin Gaye *I Heard It through the Grapevine* (1968). James Brown *Say It Loud, I'm Black and I'm Proud* (1968). Chic *Le Freak* (1978). Album: Michael Jackson *Off the Wall* (1979).

British beat
The Beatles' mixture of R and B, rock and roll and Motown gave rise to a new style. Although part of the same movement, the Rolling Stones' music was harder and closer to R and B. The line-up was based on drums, bass and two guitars, with vocal lead and harmonies.

The Beatles *Love Me Do* (1962), *Please Please Me* (1963), *Help!* (1965). The Honeycombs *Have I the Right?* (1964). The Rolling Stones *Satisfaction* (1965). The Who *My Generation* (1965).

Heavy metal
Heavy metal was amplified to great volumes, making the drums crash and the electric guitars wail. These techniques were first applied to a mixture of blues and R and B in the late 1960s.

Black Sabbath *Paranoid* (1970). Albums: Led Zeppelin *Led Zeppelin 2* (1969). Motorhead *Motorhead* (1975). Van Halen *Van Halen* (1977).

*There is more about the blues and spirituals on page 14.

Psychedelia

During the late 60s, some musicians tried to convey the effects of mind-expanding drugs through their music. They used new studio technology to achieve elaborate and exotic effects. In some cases they expanded the standard pop song to last a whole album side.

Albums: The Beach Boys *Smile* (1967). The Beatles *Sergeant Pepper* (1967). Pink Floyd *The Piper at the Gates of Dawn* (1967). Terry Riley *In C* (1968).

Glam rock

During the 70s, some rock stars cultivated extreme, fantasy images. Their music was known as glam, glitter or camp rock. The glam movement took inspiration from early 50s styles.

Gary Glitter *Rock and Roll Part 2* (1972). Albums: David Bowie *Ziggy Stardust and the Spiders from Mars* (1972). Roxy Music *Roxy Music* (1972).

Reggae

Reggae evolved in Jamaica from a mixture of calypso, mento and R and B. Many of the songs protest against social conditions and corruption. In the late 70s, Jamaican record producers invented dub. This involved using their mixing desks* to make voices and instruments zoom in and echo out over the bass and drums.

Dave and Ansel Collins *Monkey Spanner* (1971). Althea and Donna *Uptown Top Ranking* (1977). Albums: Bob Marley and the Wailers *African Herbsman* (1972). Lee Perry *Super Ape* (1978).

Punk

During the 70s, unemployment and the outlook for young people in Britain got worse. The songs and lifestyles of rich rock stars became more and more irrelevant. The punk revolution was a move back to the basics of rock: music made by young people, expressing how they felt.

The Clash *White Riot* (1977). Albums: The Sex Pistols *Never Mind the Bollocks, Here's the Sex Pistols* (1977). The Ramones *The Ramones* (1977). The Slits *Cut* (1978).

New wave and post-punk

After the first explosion, a less aggressive face of the punk generation emerged. They were musically more adventurous, many using synthesizers and drum machines.

Television *Little Johnny Jewel* (1977). Talking Heads *Psycho Killer* (1977). Blondie *Heart of Glass* (1978). Joy Division *Love will Tear Us Apart* (1980).

New Romantic

In the early 1980s, a cool and controlled style emerged in reaction to punk. The groups were called New Romantics. They used video to sell their records and their image.

Visage *Fade to Grey* (1980). Spandau Ballet *Chant No. 1* (1981). Eurythmics *Sweet Dreams* (1983).

Rap, scratch and hip hop

In the early 1980s, American club DJs began half singing and half talking over the instrumental B sides of dance records. This was called rap. Scratching involved running phrases from one record back and forth over another. Scratching over a drum machine was called hip hop.

Kurtis Blow *The Breaks* (1980). Grandmaster Flash *Grandmaster Flash and the Wheels of Steel* (1981). Malcolm McLaren *Buffalo Girls* (1983).

House music

A sampler can record and play back a sound at any pitch.** House music, named after the Warehouse Club in Chicago, developed from scratch and uses sampled sounds over fast, rhythmic, synthesized bass lines. The samples can be anything from parts of other records to news broadcasts.

Public Enemy *Don't Believe the Hype* (1988). Tone Loc *Wild Thing* (1989). Album: Twin Hype *Twin Hype* (1989).

*You can find out a bit about mixing desks on page 46.
**You can find out more about samplers on page 29.

THE ROCK BUSINESS

The rock business is a multi-million dollar industry. It provides a living for more accountants, agents and promoters than musicians. Most rock groups start small, though, arranging their own gigs in local clubs and pubs. For publicity, they might tell the local paper and put up posters.

In comparison, the chart below shows the team needed to run a major rock group's concert tour.

Arranging a concert tour

MANAGER
The group's manager hires an agent and a tour manager.

AGENT
The agent approaches promoters and produces a schedule for the tour.

TOUR MANAGER
The tour manager arranges transportation, accommodations and equipment.

PROMOTERS
A promoter in each location hires the concert hall and security staff. They organize ticket sales and local publicity.

ROAD CREW
The road crew move, maintain and install equipment. There are also sound, lighting and video effects technicians.

TOUR ACCOUNTANT
The accountant collects ticket money from promoters, pays the crew, hotel bills and so on.

SECURITY STAFF
The tour manager's security staff include bodyguards for the group if necessary.

PUBLICISTS
Publicists meet with the group's record company and set up interviews with the local press and TV.

The manager's job

A group's manager arranges concerts and sets up recording contracts. The manager needs to be sympathetic to the group's music and image, while steering them towards a wider public.

The record industry

A major record company might spend so much money making and promoting a record that it needs to sell at least 100,000 copies before it makes a profit.

The record companies Polygram, CBS, EMI, WEA and BMG control most of the world market in recorded music.

Small record companies cannot afford to spend as much on promotion as a big company. Instead, they specialize and build up a reputation for a particular kind of music.

The company's A and R (artistes and repertoire) team are in charge of finding new talent. They receive hundreds of demo tapes a week.

Videos

Since the mid-80s, hardly a record is made by a big company without a video to promote it. The video can cost more to make than the record itself. Record companies think the cost is worthwhile because a TV broadcast of the video reaches a much larger audience than a radio broadcast of the record.

Video tape is cheaper and quicker to edit than ordinary film. It is easier to produce special effects on video and to make copies for distribution to TV stations.

JAZZ

Jazz musicians almost never play a tune the same way twice. Most jazz is improvised (made up on the spot). The musicians make up their own version of a tune. This makes jazz different from rock or classical music where the notes are fixed by the composer.

Jazz is like a musical language. When the musicians play, they talk to each other in jazz language. They talk about the tune but say different things about it.

The structure of jazz

Most jazz is based on a tune or theme. The tune might be made up specially, or it might be a popular tune.

If you listen to the tune carefully at this stage, it is easier to understand what happens next.

The soloist plays around with the theme, adding and changing notes.

Most jazz consists of a series of choruses.

First, the band members play the tune or theme through. They play the melody and the harmonies that go with it. This version is usually quite simple.

Then, musicians take turns to improvise solos based on the theme. The others play the same harmonies and rhythm as the first time.

At the end, the whole band plays the theme through again to round everything off.
Each time the tune is played through it is called a chorus.

Jazz instruments

Some front line instruments

A jazz group, or line-up, has two parts. These are the rhythm section and the front line.

Front-line instruments are those that play a solo during the piece.

The rhythm section keeps a steady pulse. It also plays the tune's harmonies for the front line to improvise over.

Instruments may swap roles. For example, you often hear a drum or a double bass solo. A pianist can play a rhythm and a solo part at the same time.

Some rhythm section instruments

Clarinet

Trumpet

Trombone

Saxophone

Bass guitar

Double bass

Right hand: solo.

Left hand: rhythm.

Piano

Drums

Rhythm and syncopation

Most rhythms have a regular pulse, or beat. The picture below shows a rhythm which has two beats in each group, or bar*. The first beat in a bar is usually the strongest. You can hear this by saying "ONE two ONE two".

Some music places the stress elsewhere in the bar. This is called syncopation. This simple syncopated rhythm places the stress on the second beat.

Jazz has complex syncopation. The accents might fall between the beats of the bar. This causes an interesting tension between the steady pulse and the syncopated rhythm.

Jazz swing

Cool	Laid back	Loose-jointed	Elastic	Easy

Jazz began as dance music. It has a rhythmic quality called swing which makes you want to tap your feet and move to it. The words above describe swing.

Jazz swing comes from the way musicians play syncopated rhythms. They might play a note just before or after the beat. This gives a flexible, relaxed feel.

Jazz rhythm and tap

Tap dancers used to be called hoofers. "Hoof" is slang for "foot".

To imagine jazz rhythm, think of tap dancers. They can sound just like jazz drummers. The first tap dancers were black entertainers who danced to jazz.

Jam sessions

In a jam session, musicians play together, usually without an audience. They try out tunes, rhythms and harmonies. Most jazz evolves during jam sessions.

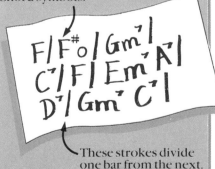

The name "jam session" was first given to all-night competitions between local and visiting jazz musicians. These took place in Kansas City in the 1920s.

Composing jazz

Most composers belong to a band and work on their compositions during jam sessions.

Composer: tune, rhythm, harmonies, speed (tempo)

Musicians: final choice of notes and style of playing while improvising.

Jazz composers do not write down every note. They just provide an outline consisting of a tune and harmonies. They might also provide passages to link choruses and begin or end the piece. Soloists improvise within this structure.

Each chorus is 12 bars long. Numbers show how many bars* are in each section. "Ch" stands for chorus.

Trumpet and sax improvise in turn, backed by a drum.

The theme is repeated at the end.

This shows which notes to end on.

A composer might produce a structure called a head arrangement. It is so-called because musicians memorize it, or only jot down a few notes. (There is an example above.) A big band may need head arrangements to avoid chaos.

Writing jazz down

When jazz musicians improvise, they base what they play on the harmonies that go with a tune.

Chord symbols.

These strokes divide one bar from the next.

They may jot down harmonies in a shorthand known as chord symbols. A chord is a group of notes played together. The symbols tell the musician which chords accompany a tune.

You can find out more about chords on pages 51 and 52.

*Bars are explained in more detail on page 18 and pages 48-49.
**This stands for tenor saxophone.

9

THE STORY OF JAZZ

Jazz music is only about 90 years old. It has been through many changes, though. You can still hear most forms of jazz, either on record or live in pubs and jazz clubs.

Jazz began early this century in New Orleans, Louisiana in the southern USA.

Jazz roots: 1900-1920

Many different nationalities lived in or travelled through the port of New Orleans. Each had its own music. The picture shows some of the mixture of music that gave birth to jazz.

◀ Ragtime. This was a form of piano music played in bars and drinking clubs.

European ballroom dance music. This was very popular in the 19th century. ▶

◀ Blues. This was a type of black folk music. It developed among the descendants of slaves.

Most early jazz bands had six members. ▼

French military band music. (Louisiana was also once a French colony.) ▼

Spanish folk music. (Louisiana was once ruled by Spain.) ▶

NEW ORLEANS

Jazz was invented by black musicians. The tunes and styles were passed on by ear. The musicians did not have to be able to read music.

Early jazz bands used folk and popular tunes as themes. The cornet usually led the melody. Other instruments improvised intricate patterns around it.

Cornet player.

1920s: the Jazz Age

In the early 1920s, many jazz musicians left New Orleans. They went to try jazz out on other cities, such as Chicago.

As the 1930s drew near, many musicians went to New York. This was the centre for radio, recording and entertainment.

1920s jazz was called New Orleans or Dixieland jazz.

New Orleans jazz is still played. It is sometimes called Traditional or Trad jazz.

The 1920s were called the Jazz Age. Dancing and listening to jazz was a craze among both black and white people.

THE GREAT LAKES

By 1930, New York was the jazz centre of the world.

NEW YORK

CHICAGO

NEW ORLEANS

The first jazz record was made in 1917 and the recording industry developed rapidly. Radio broadcasting began in the early 1920s. These things helped jazz to spread.

1920s jazz profile: Louis Armstrong

Louis Armstrong changed the sound of jazz. Earlier, the whole band played for most of the time, improvising around each other. Louis was so brilliant that he was allowed to play solos. Since then, jazz has been based on solos.

1930s: the Swing Era

In the 1930s, bands got bigger so that they could be heard in large ballrooms. The band used written music or head arrangements* and took turns to improvise solos.

1930s jazz profile: Duke Ellington

Duke Ellington led a big band for 45 years. He was a great jazz composer.

As well as composing lots of original music, he wrote his own versions of existing tunes. These are called arrangements.

The style they played was called swing. It was smoother and simpler than earlier jazz. The period between 1935 and 1940 is known as the Swing Era.

The bands were called swing bands or big bands. Many big bands contained a singer or two. Swing singers sang in a smooth, crooning style.

1940s jazz profile: Charlie Parker

Charlie Parker was the main inventor of a style called be-bop. His impact was as great as Louis Armstrong's had been. His style was so new that some people thought he was playing wrong notes.

1940s: hot and cool jazz

Some musicians found swing dull. They experimented with rhythm and harmony. The result was be-bop, or modern jazz. It was not meant for dancing.

Be-bop was jazz for small bands. Like early jazz, its inventors were black.

In the late 40s, the cool school developed in reaction to fiery, energetic be-bop. It was gentler and less emotional.

Trumpeter Miles Davis was a cool school pioneer.

1950s

You couldn't dance to 1940s and 50s jazz. Instead, people danced to rhythm and blues or rock and roll.**

A style called West Coast jazz developed in California. It grew out of the cool school. It was precise, relaxed and more impersonal than be-bop.

Some people still preferred the expressive and exciting be-bop to West Coast jazz. An even more energetic and tough style, called hard bop, emerged. This continued the be-bop tradition by experimenting with rhythm and changes of *tempo* (speed).

1950s jazz profile: Art Blakey

Art Blakey, a drummer, founded a black group called the Jazz Messengers. They played hard bop. He studied and used real African rhythms. This made his music exciting and vigorous.

*See page 9 for more about head arrangements.
**There is more about rhythm and blues and rock and roll on pages 4-5

1960s: free jazz

The main new jazz style of the 1960s was free jazz. It ignored earlier rules about harmony and chorus structure. At first, many people disliked it because it was hard to make sense of it.

The name free jazz caused confusion at some concerts: people thought they didn't have to pay.

1960s jazz profile: Ornette Coleman

Ornette Coleman thought each note had a special quality. Notes could be put together in any order to build an effect.

1970s: jazz funk or fusion

In the 70s, jazz and rock blended in a style called jazz-funk or fusion. Musicians made up jazzy solos over rock rhythms, using both jazz and rock instruments.

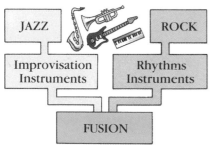

One fusion group was called Weather Report. Their music was improvised so it was changeable and unpredictable, like weather.

1980s: retrospective jazz

Wynton Marsalis uses a similar style to Miles Davis. ▶

◀ Courtney Pine follows John Coltrane's style.

In the 1980s, some musicians took existing jazz styles and developed them in their own way. This is retrospective jazz. It means using an old style to say new things.

Contemporary concert jazz

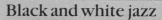

You need to concentrate hard to enjoy this sort of music.

This sort of jazz is improvised but is influenced by modern classical composers. It is played in classical concert halls. The line-up may include any kind of instrument.

Jazz singers

BAM-BAM
BA-LOO-BAH
DOO-BY
      DOO-BY
WAH-WAH

Louis Armstrong was the first to record a form of improvised singing on 26 February 1926. It was called scat singing. It consisted of tuneful, rhythmic babbling. Swing band singers, though, had to sing what the composer or arranger wanted.

Billie Holiday's best records were made with small bands, using head arrangements. ▶

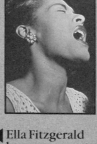

◀ Ella Fitzgerald became a great ballad singer, recording with large orchestras.

Early jazz bands accompanied singers in popular songs and the blues. Two famous singers were Billie Holiday and Ella Fitzgerald. They sang with big and small bands in the 1930s.

Black and white jazz

Until the 1940s, a band with both black and white musicians was rare. White audiences objected, most of all in the southern USA. Black musicians were paid less than whites.

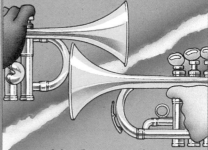

One of the first mixed recording sessions was set up by Louis Armstrong in 1929.

JAZZ TO LISTEN TO

Types of jazz are so varied that you may like some very much and others not at all. Here are some suggestions for performers to listen to in the different categories. There are also suggestions for particular tracks or albums to look out for.

New Orleans (Trad) jazz

King Oliver's Creole Jazz Band .... *Dippermouth Blues*
Louis Armstrong's Hot Five .... *Heebie Jeebies*
Jelly Roll Morton (pianist) .... *The Chant*
Bix Beiderbecke (cornet) .... *Singin' the Blues*
Sidney Bechet (clarinet/sax) .... *Shake It and Break It*

The top cornet or trumpet player in New Orleans was called "King". A challenger was called "Kid".

This contains the first scat singing on record.

Bix Beiderbecke died aged 27, having dominated white jazz in the late 1920s.

Swing

Duke Ellington (pianist) .... *Harlem Air Shaft*
Count Basie (pianist) .... *Tickle Toe*
Billie Holiday (singer) .... *Me, Myself and I*
Coleman Hawkins (tenor sax) ....*Body and Soul*

Coleman Hawkins was probably the first to play jazz on the tenor sax.

Be-bop

Charlie Parker (sax) .... *Cool Blues*
Dizzy Gillespie (trumpet) .... *The Champ*
Thelonious Monk (pianist) ....*Round About Midnight*

Gillespie was a friend of Charlie Parker and a key developer of be-bop.

Thelonious Monk's style consisted of few notes with complex rhythms and unusual harmonies.

Cool jazz

Miles Davis (trumpet) .... *Godchild*
Stan Getz (tenor sax) ....*Moonlight in Vermont*

West coast

Dave Brubeck (piano) .... *Take Five*
Gerry Mulligan (baritone sax) .... *Lullaby of the Leaves*
Art Pepper (alto sax) ....*Art Pepper Plus Eleven* (album)

This has five beats in a bar. Most music has two, three or four beats in a bar.*

By the age of 15, Art Pepper was playing in all-night clubs in Los Angeles.

Hard bop

Art Blakey (drummer) ....*A Night at Birdland* (album)
Sonny Rollins (tenor sax) ....*Saxophone Colossus* (album)
Horace Silver (pianist) ....*The Preacher*

Horace Silver was the first pianist with Art Blakey's Jazz Messengers before becoming a bandleader himself.

Free jazz

Ornette Coleman (sax) .... *Change of the Century* (album)
John Coltrane (sax) .... *Ascension* (album)

Fusion

Herbie Hancock (keyboards) .... *Headhunter* (album)
Weather Report .... *Heavy Weather* (album)

Retrospective jazz

Courtney Pine (sax) ....*Journey to the Urge Within* (album)
Wynton Marsalis (trumpet) .... *Black Codes from the Underground* (album)

*You can find out about time signatures and bars on pages 18 and 48.

FOLK AND ETHNIC MUSIC

Before TV, records, radio or cinema existed, people created their own entertainment. They did this by getting together and dancing or singing. The music they played is called folk or ethnic music. It is a country's traditional music. Each generation teaches the songs and dances to the next.

Folk dancing

Folk dancers usually perform certain sequences of movements. These may once have had a religious meaning. In some parts of the world, such as Bali, dancers re-enact legends and stories of gods and goddesses.

Folk song

The original purpose of a folk song may be forgotten but it may still be sung for fun. Here are the roots of some types of song.

Work songs

WHAT SHALL WE DO WITH THE DRUNKEN SAILOR- EARLY IN THE MORNING?

Work songs helped people keep going during hard labour. The rhythms helped them work as a team.

Sailors had sea shanties for hauling the anchor, raising sails and so on.

Blues

The blues were sung by black people in the southern USA in the 19th century. Many were about the misery of their lives.

BLACK MOUNTAIN PEOPLE ARE BAD AS THEY CAN BE. BLACK MOUNTAIN PEOPLE ARE BAD AS THEY CAN BE. THEY USES GUNPOWDER JUST TO SWEETEN THEIR TEA.

Children's play songs

Children sing songs to go with dances or games. Though cheerful, many were originally about politics or disasters. The song below is about the symptoms of the plague in England in 1665.

RING-A-RING-A-ROSES A POCKETFUL OF POSIES ATISHOO ATISHOO WE ALL FALL DOWN

Spirituals

White slave owners in the southern USA made their slaves become Christians. The slaves re-worked hymns into spirituals. These echoed the rhythm and song styles of West African music.

SWING LOW, SWEET CHARIOT

COMING FOR TO CARRY ME HOME

This spiritual has a call and response pattern: everyone joins in on alternate lines.

Ballads

Ballads tell stories. They began as unaccompanied solos. Today, they are often sung by groups with instruments. Common themes for ballads are heroic acts, tragedies and love stories.

Some folk instruments

Folk instruments are mostly cheap and easy to carry. Here are some folk instruments and where they might be used.

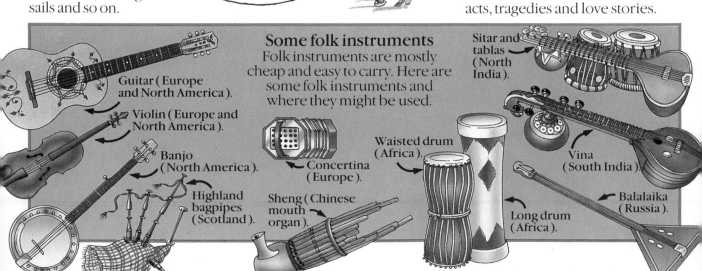

Guitar (Europe and North America).

Violin (Europe and North America).

Banjo (North America).

Highland bagpipes (Scotland).

Concertina (Europe).

Sheng (Chinese mouth organ).

Waisted drum (Africa).

Long drum (Africa).

Sitar and tablas (North India).

Vina (South India).

Balalaika (Russia).

How folk music develops

In the past, people travelled less than nowadays. Styles of folk music developed separately in different places.

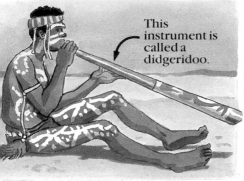

This instrument is called a didgeridoo.

The American Indians mostly used pipes and percussion.

English, French, Dutch and Spanish colonies were set up in the 17th century.

Spanish conquerors invaded South America in the 16th century.

The African slave trade lasted for 200 years until slavery was abolished in 1865.

For thousands of years, the only inhabitants of Australia were the Aborigines. Their music was untouched by other styles until European settlers arrived 200 years ago.

When people did travel, for instance as explorers, convicts or slaves, they took their music with them. American folk music is a mixture of styles brought by settlers and invaders.

African slaves brought their rhythms and use of percussion. European settlers brought tunes and dances. They introduced the violin, guitar, harp and brass military band instruments.

Folk now

Folk music is "do-it-yourself music", so it is cheap. This is why it is still a living style in many poor countries. Richer countries have access to all sorts of music through records and radio. In these countries, folk has mostly been replaced though it is kept alive by fans at folk clubs and folk festivals.

The folk group on the left, Steeleye Span, were in the British charts in the 1970s. They used electric instruments. Some fans think that folk is a traditional style and musicians should not use modern instruments. Others accept that folk changes with the times: modern instruments bring it up to date.

Folk and nationality

Folk music is often used as a tourist attraction. It provides a foreign flavour. It also gives people on vacation an experience which they will not find back home.

Folk music to listen to

You could see if your local record library has any records by these musicians in stock. If not, the library might order some for you.

Egypt: Soliman Gamil.
Gambia (West Africa): Dembo Konte or Toumani Diabate.
Britain: Martin Carthy.
Ireland: The Chieftains.
Spain: Mocedades.
Greece: Nana Mouskouri.
France: Alan Itwell.
South America: Inti Illimani.
Blues (USA): Big Bill Broonzy.
Bluegrass (a white American folk style): Lester Flatt and Earl Scruggs.

Folk-influenced music

Bhangra is a type of Indian folk music, jazzed up. It consists of traditional tunes and words, with disco rhythms. Two groups that play bhangra are Heera and Holle Holle.

EARLY MUSIC

Most classical music after the 17th century consists of a tune with accompanying harmonies. Early medieval music, though, consisted of a single tune with no harmonies. The change from one style to the other began during the Middle Ages, or medieval times. (This period began towards the end of the 5th century and lasted until the 14th century.) You can see how styles changed by looking at singing styles in the early Christian Church.

Medieval church music

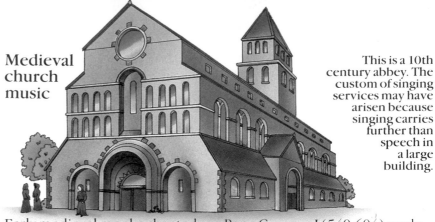

This is a 10th century abbey. The custom of singing services may have arisen because singing carries further than speech in a large building.

Early medieval monks chanted their church services. They all sang the same tune. This was called plainsong or plainchant. This type of single-line music is called monophony.

Pope Gregory I (540-604) made rules about how plainsong should be sung. There were almost 3000 Gregorian Chants. Many Catholic services still include some plainsong.

Part-singing in church

During the Middle Ages, groups of people began to sing different notes at the same time. This is called part-singing. You can follow some of the early stages in its development below.

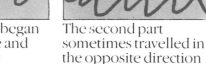

The drone may have first been sung by monks who could not sing in tune.

Cantus firmus

Drone

One group sang the tune, or *cantus firmus*. Another chanted a low note, called a drone.

Ninth century

The second part began to follow the rise and fall of the *cantus firmus*.

Eleventh century

The second part sometimes travelled in the opposite direction to the *cantus firmus*.

Late twelfth century

The different tunes and rhythms blend together.

Two or more parts moved independently. Each was a separate tune. This is called polyphony.

Music for entertainment

From around the 10th century, professional male musicians provided music for entertainment. Some travelled about the countryside, playing in rich households for money and food or entertaining in town squares. They wrote songs and accompanied themselves on musical instruments.

Jongleurs were acrobats and jugglers as well as musicians. They often provided music for folk dances.

Minstrels were rather more respectable than *jongleurs*. They sang romantic songs.

In central and northern France, minstrels were called *trouvères*.

Southern French minstrels were called *troubadours*.

Minnesingers, (love singers), were German minstrels.

Jongleurs

Recorder

Minstrel

Lute

Trouvère

Harp

Troubadour

Viol

Minnesinger

Music in the Renaissance

The Renaissance* began in 14th century Italy. New ideas about art, architecture and music, inspired by Ancient Greek culture, spread over Europe over the next 200 years. Some of today's attitudes to music originated in the Renaissance.

Small groups of people sang polyphonic part songs called madrigals**.

● In the Middle Ages, musical instruments were mostly played by professionals. In the Renaissance, learning to read and play music became part of a good education.

● Composers began to write for particular instruments and to balance and contrast instrumental tones. This is how orchestral groups originated.

Then

Now

● Composers also began to write music for instruments on their own, without singers.

● People began to regard music as an art form. This meant that it had an artistic value as well as a practical purpose for worship or entertainment.

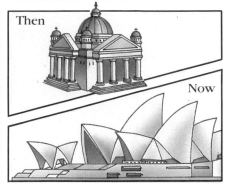

Then

Now

● People listened to music in chapels and cathedrals. There were no concert halls.

Renaissance instruments

A consort of viols.

Wealthy families owned sets of instruments, called consorts or chests. These consisted of four or more of the same instrument, each with a different range of pitch. A group of instruments from more than one set was called a broken consort.

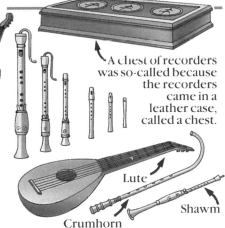

A chest of recorders was so-called because the recorders came in a leather case, called a chest.

Lute

Crumhorn

Shawm

Other Renaissance instruments

Early music to listen to

Palestrina (c.1525-1594) wrote many polyphonic settings of the Roman Catholic Mass, such as the *Missa Papae Marcelli* (*Mass of Pope Marcellus*). For a work based on plainsong, listen to his *Assumpta est Maria*, especially the *Antiphon*.

Giovanni Gabrieli (1557-1612) produced canzonas. A canzona was the main 16th century form of instrumental composition.

The main medieval polyphonic song form was called a motet. There were religious and non-religious (secular) motets. Here are some composers who wrote motets:

Guillaume Dufay (c.1400-1474). Thomas Tallis (c.1505-1585) wrote a 40-part motet called *Spem in Alium*. It was written for eight five-part choirs, one voice per part.
Guillaume de Machaut (1300-1377) composed motets and a polyphonic Mass, called *La Messe de Notre Dame*. Josquin des Prez (c.1445-1521) wrote motets and Masses.

Writing music down

Accents show the general rise and fall of the melody.

An early staff had four lines.

Each line or space represents a note.

The first attempt to write music down was in the 7th century. The system was vague and today it is impossible to follow. The signs were called neumes.

In the 11th century, a monk called Guido d'Arezzo found a better way to write music down. He used sets of lines called staffs. Over the page, you can see how music is written today.

*"Renaissance" means "rebirth".
**You can find out more about madrigals on page 37.

WRITING MUSIC DOWN

A composer writes music down so that it can be played exactly as he or she intended. The system used today developed in Europe, alongside polyphony (see pages 16-17). It helped people sing or play the right notes so that different parts fit together.

If you cannot read music, this page will give you the very basics. There is more information about reading and writing music on pages 48-53.

Rhythm and pitch

Most musical rhythms consist of a pattern of sounds around a steady pulse. The pulse consists of regular beats. A sound might last for a whole beat, a fraction of a beat or for several beats.

The pulse is divided into groups of beats called bars. Numbers at the beginning of each line of music tell you how many beats there are in each bar. The numbers are called a time signature.

This time signature tells you that there are two crotchet beats in each bar. (The four stands for crotchets, or quarter notes.) You can hear the pulse by counting ONE two ONE two. The first beat in the bar is normally stronger than the other beats.

Each set of five lines is called a staff. The signs at the beginning of the staffs are called the treble and bass clefs (explained below).

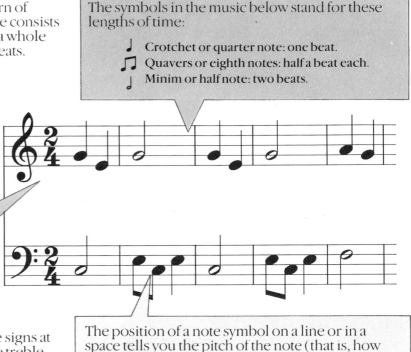

The symbols in the music below stand for these lengths of time:

♩ Crotchet or quarter note: one beat.
♫ Quavers or eighth notes: half a beat each.
♩ Minim or half note: two beats.

The position of a note symbol on a line or in a space tells you the pitch of the note (that is, how high or low it is).

Putting notes on the staff

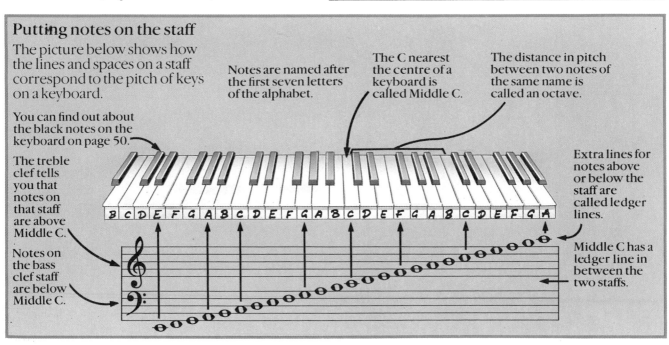

The picture below shows how the lines and spaces on a staff correspond to the pitch of keys on a keyboard.

You can find out about the black notes on the keyboard on page 50.

The treble clef tells you that notes on that staff are above Middle C.

Notes on the bass clef staff are below Middle C.

Notes are named after the first seven letters of the alphabet.

The C nearest the centre of a keyboard is called Middle C.

The distance in pitch between two notes of the same name is called an octave.

Extra lines for notes above or below the staff are called ledger lines.

Middle C has a ledger line in between the two staffs.

SETS OF NOTES: SCALES

Most music is made up of notes chosen from a set called a scale. There are lots of different sorts of scale. Music from some parts of the world may sound quite strange to you. This can be because it is based on different scales from those you are used to.

Distances between notes

The smallest distance, or interval, between two notes on a keyboard is called a semitone. Two semitones make one tone. A semitone is the smallest interval you can write on a staff.

⌢ = tone ⌢ = semitone

Some music, such as Indian music, uses intervals smaller than a semitone. This means that this sort of music cannot be written on a staff. Instead, it is memorized, or improvised round memorized patterns of notes.

Major scales

Since the Renaissance, most Western music has been based on scales called major and minor scales. They go from one note to the same note an octave (eight notes) higher.

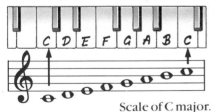

Scale of C major.

The simplest major scale which you can play on a keyboard starts on the note C. This scale uses only the white notes on the keyboard. A tune based on notes from the scale of C major is said to be in the key of C major.

Pattern of tones and semitones in C major.

⌢ = tone ⌢ = semitone

Building major scales

A major scale can start on any note but it must have the same pattern of tones and semitones as the scale of C major. This means that other major scales, such as G major on the right, have to include black notes on a keyboard. You can find out about other major scales and about minor scales on page 50.

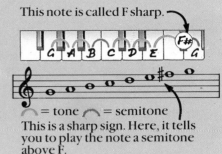

This note is called F sharp.

⌢ = tone ⌢ = semitone

This is a sharp sign. Here, it tells you to play the note a semitone above F.

Other types of scale

If you have access to a keyboard, you could try playing the scales below. You could compare them to the scale of C major. A scale containing five notes is called a pentatonic scale. Most Chinese and Japanese music is based on pentatonic scales.

⌢ = tone
⌢ = semitone
⌢ = 1½ tones

The black notes on a keyboard form a Chinese pentatonic scale. So do the notes above.

Intervals of two tones.

A lot of Japanese music is built on the two pentatonic scales above.

A chromatic scale* includes all 12 black and white notes within an octave.

A whole tone scale* has six equal steps of a tone each.

Ancient scales

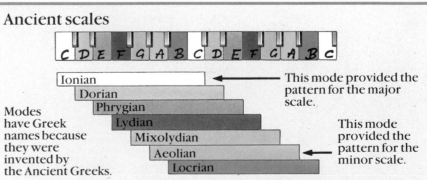

This mode provided the pattern for the major scale.

Modes have Greek names because they were invented by the Ancient Greeks.

This mode provided the pattern for the minor scale.

Eastern music, some western folk music and much medieval music is based on Ancient Greek scales called modes. These only use the white notes on the keyboard.

Each mode begins on a different note and has a Greek name. You could try playing them to see how the patterns of tones and semitones make them sound different from each other.

---

*Some 20th century composers used the whole tone and chromatic scales (see page 26).

BAROQUE MUSIC

Between about 1600 and 1750, a new style of European music emerged. Instead of having several tunes which fit together (called polyphony), it had one main tune. This was accompanied by bass and harmony parts.

Some composers still wrote polyphonic music. During this time, they began to base it on a framework of chords.

The word baroque means elaborately decorated. It describes the architecture and art of the time as well as the music.

A baroque orchestra

The size of a baroque orchestra depended on the instruments available. Violins usually played the tune: their bright tone made it stand out. A cello, double bass or bassoon played the bass part. A harpsichord played harmonies. There might also be violas, oboes, horns, trumpets and drums.

Most composers did not write out the harmony part in full. Instead, the harpsichord music consisted of the bass part with numbers written on it. This was called a figured bass or *basso continuo*. The numbers stood for chords. The musician improvised a harmony based on the chords. Most figured basses have now been filled in and printed. You could still learn how to play from a figured bass but it requires a lot of skill.

Violins formed the main body of the orchestra.

A figured bass allowed the musician some freedom of interpretation.

How baroque composers lived

Renaissance and baroque composers were employed by the nobility or the Church. They had to write music to order for religious services or for entertainment. This system was called patronage.

They might have to write operas* and ballets to entertain the court.

King Louis XIV of France was a keen ballet dancer.

They composed cantatas and chorales* for church choirs and congregations.

Bach and Handel

Two famous composers were Johann Sebastian Bach (1685-1750) and George Frideric Handel (1685-1759). They were both German and the same age but their lives and music were different.

Bach never left Germany. He worked in churches and chapels as well as courts.

Handel studied in Italy. He worked in Germany and England for princes and dukes.

Bach's music did not make him rich, even though he was a genius.

Handel successfully followed the changing musical fashions.

After Bach died, most of his work was forgotten until it was rediscovered in the 19th century.

Handel's music had a wide reputation. People carried on performing it after his death.

When listening to Bach, try to pick out the other parts besides the tune. They all fit together perfectly.

You may find Handel's music easier to listen to at first than some of Bach's. It was meant for a wider audience.

*You can find out more about opera and choral music on pages 36-40.

Baroque musical forms

During this time, the quality of instruments and standard of playing improved. An orchestra could provide interesting combinations of instruments.

Composers were inspired to write longer works so certain frameworks emerged. Most consisted of linked sections. Below are some baroque forms.

Sonata

A sonata contained contrasting sections, or movements. There were two types of sonata. A *sonata da camera*, or chamber sonata, was based on dance tunes. The picture on the left shows a *sonata da camera* being played at a private party. A *sonata da chiesa*, or church sonata, was more solemn.

This is a baroque cathedral in which a *sonata da chiesa* might have been played. It shows some ornate baroque architecture.

Suite

A suite was a set of dance tunes but people were not meant to dance to them. The tunes took their rhythm and style from the dances after which they were named.

Tunes for these dances might be included in a suite: *allemande, courante, sarabande, minuet* and *gigue.*

Concerto grosso

Concertante strings might include:

2 Violins

0 Violas

1 Cello

Ripieno strings might include:

10

2

3

Concerto Grosso
IN F MINOR
SOLO VIOLIN
EBENEZER ROCKENHOSS
CONTINUO
BERTHA BULLSBLOOD : CELLO
CELIA SPOTZ : HARPSICHORD
with
The MANGELNOTE
PHILHARMONIC ORCHESTRA

The instruments used may be listed on a record sleeve.

A concerto grosso had three or more movements. The orchestra was divided into two groups. A small group of strings called the *concertante* or *soli* strings played a solo part. This was contrasted with a larger group called the *ripieno* strings. The *soli* group might include wind or *basso continuo* instruments.

Prelude and fugue

A prelude is an introduction to a fugue. A fugue is polyphonic and is usually for a keyboard. It begins with a short tune played in a solo line. One by one, other parts enter and take up the tune. The parts then play different versions of the tune. They weave round each other, overlapping and making complex patterns with the tune.

Bach composed lots of fugues for the organ.

CLASSICAL MUSIC

During the second half of the 18th century, composers found a new audience: wealthier members of the public would pay to attend concerts. Musicians began to make a living without depending totally on patronage.

In art and architecture as well as music, people liked formal, balanced structures. A lighter, more graceful style replaced the grandeur and intricacy of baroque music. Music written for concerts and church services between about 1750 and 1820 is called Classical music.

The symphony

A new musical form called a symphony developed. This is a long work in three or four movements for an orchestra. The composer uses its length to develop and express ideas on a large scale, contrasting different instrumental groups.

Trumpets, horns and drums were added for special effects.

The instruments in a Classical orchestra varied but this one is fairly typical. The harpsichord and *basso continuo** went out of use. Other instruments took on the task of playing harmonies. There were usually between 25 and 40 members. A symphony orchestra today might have over 100 instruments.**

The concerto

The baroque concerto grosso developed into the Classical concerto. This is in three movements. It is written for a soloist and orchestra. A concerto shows off a soloist's skill. A brilliant soloist is called a virtuoso.

Towards the end of a movement, the soloist may play alone for a few minutes. This is called a *cadenza*. It is the soloist's chance to end with a flourish. Classical soloists often improvised the *cadenzas*. Later composers wrote them in themselves.

Overtures

An overture is a short piece for an orchestra. Overtures were performed before an opera or play to put the audience in the right mood. Some were written for their own sake, unconnected to a play or opera.

Variations

Theme | Theme turned upside down. | New rhythm.

Theme decorated. | New time signature. | Change of key.

A set of variations begins with a theme. The theme is repeated several times but each time it is changed or varied. It may have a different rhythm or mood.

The picture above shows some of the ways in which a theme can be adapted. A composer tries to alter a theme's characteristics without losing its identity.

* See page 20 for more about the basso continuo.
** There is more about a symphony orchestra on page 23.

The Classical sonata

An instrumental group playing a Classical sonata.

The sonata developed into a form with three or four movements. Many Classical sonatas are for small groups of instruments. A symphony is a sonata for an orchestra.

Chamber music

Viola

Cello

A lot of chamber music is Classical. This is a string quartet.

Two violins

Two=duo
Three=trio
Four=quartet
Five=quintet
Six=sextet
Seven=septet
Eight=octet

Chamber music is played by a small group. You may not hear a wide variety of tones. Instead, listen to how the parts weave round each other and pass the tune between them.

All the instruments play most of the time and are equally important. A piece of chamber music may be called after the number of instruments it is written for, as shown above.

Clapping at a concert

You are not supposed to clap between the movements of a concerto, symphony or sonata. It might spoil the mood and distract the musicians.

The invention of the piano

The first piano, or pianoforte, was made in the early 18th century. Pianos soon became more popular than harpsichords: you could play loudly or softly on them. *Piano* means soft and *forte* means loud in Italian.

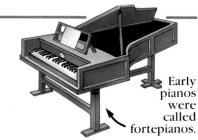

Early pianos were called fortepianos.

Classical composers and patronage

Mozart (1756-1791) wrote his first sonata at the age of five. As an adult he refused to conform to the ideas of his patrons so he was often out of work. Some of his music was too complex for the public, so he could not make a proper living from concerts, either. He died young, in poverty.

Haydn (1732-1809) was born 24 years before Mozart but died 18 years after him. He spent most of his working life in the Hungarian court of Prince Esterhazy under the system of patronage*. Towards the end of his life, he found the pressure of producing music to order rather a burden.

Beethoven (1770-1827) bridged the gap between the Classical period and the next, which is called the Romantic era. He was the first composer to succeed in making a living without the support of a patron.

*Patronage is explained on page 20.

Classical music to listen to

Haydn:
Surprise Symphony No. 94 in G Major.
Trumpet Concerto in E Flat.

Mozart:
Symphony No. 39 in E Flat, No. 40 in G Minor and *No. 41 in C.* (Mozart wrote these symphonies in six weeks during 1788.)
Overtures to the operas *The Magic Flute* and *The Marriage of Figaro.*
Piano Sonata No. 11 in A Major.

Beethoven:
Symphony No. 5.
Violin Concerto. (The *cadenza* usually played in this was made up by the violinist Kreisler. *Fidelio* and *Egmont* overtures.

Chamber music

Haydn:
Quartet in C Opus 76 No. 3 (*Emperor Quartet*). The German national anthem is based on the theme from this quartet.

Mozart:
Clarinet Quintet in A Major.
Oboe Quartet in F Major.

Beethoven:
Archduke Trio.

ROMANTIC MUSIC

During the 19th century, composers began to use music to express feelings and even to tell stories. They ignored Classical forms or used them loosely, letting the emotional content shape the music. Describing emotions became more important than musical elegance.

Painters and writers also began to use their art to convey personal feelings and experience. This movement in art and music was called the Romantic movement. It lasted until the 20th century.

The orchestra

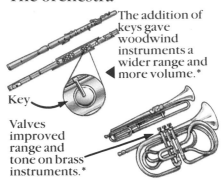

The addition of keys gave woodwind instruments a wider range and more volume.*

Key

Valves improved range and tone on brass instruments.*

The orchestra grew and instruments were improved in order to fill large new concert halls with sound.

Romantic composers wanted

The piano was given an iron frame instead of a wooden one. This could stand tighter, thicker strings which gave a louder, fuller sound.*

New members of the orchestra:

Piccolo

Cor anglais

Bass clarinet

to convey a wide range of emotions and atmospheres. New and improved instruments helped them to achieve more contrasts in tone and volume.

Musical stories and pictures

Music which tells a story or paints a picture is called programme music. The name comes from the notes, or programme, that some

composers wrote to explain their music. Long works of programme music are called symphonic, or tone, poems.

Tchaikovsky's *1812 Overture* describes Napoleon's retreat from Moscow.

Scheherezade by Rimsky-Korsakov is based on the *Arabian Nights* tales.

Harriet Smithson

Berlioz (1803-1869) composed a symphonic poem, *Symphonie Fantastique*, to describe his love for an actress, Harriet Smithson. He invited her to a performance and later she married him. Berlioz was good at composing for huge orchestras.

Mussorgsky's *Pictures at an Exhibition* describes ten paintings.

Beethoven's *Pastoral Symphony* is about life in the country.

You cannot follow a story or tell what a picture looks like by listening to music. Instead, the composer tries to arouse feelings similar to how the picture or story might make you feel. There may be clues to the nature of the music in the title.

Composers created atmosphere by their use of *tempo*, rhythm, harmony or instrumentation. Rapid or unexpected changes of key might create a feeling of suspense or turmoil. Strange combinations of notes create a sense of uneasiness or dread.

The devil and Paganini

Paganini (1782-1840) was a brilliant virtuoso violinist. People found his talent so incredible that rumours started which said that he was in league with the devil. Paganini did not object because the rumours made him even more famous.

Nationalism

Before the 19th century, European music was mostly dominated by certain centres. Italy was the centre in Handel's time and Vienna in Mozart's time. Musical styles throughout Europe were influenced by fashions in these centres.

Certain Romantic composers rebelled against this and began to express national identity in their music. This was called the Nationalist movement. They borrowed folk rhythms, harmonies and tunes to give their music a national flavour.

This map shows where some Nationalist composers came from.

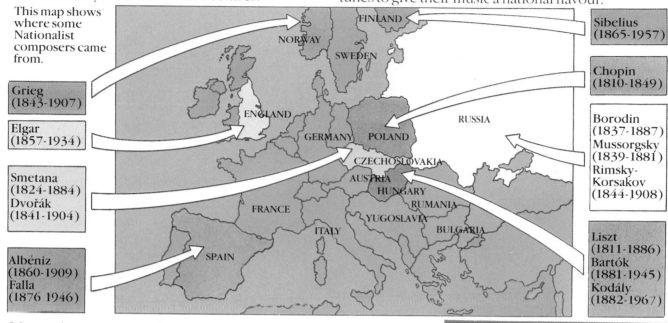

Grieg
(1843-1907)

Elgar
(1857-1934)

Smetana
(1824-1884)
Dvořák
(1841-1904)

Albéniz
(1860-1909)
Falla
(1876 1946)

Sibelius
(1865-1957)

Chopin
(1810-1849)

Borodin
(1837-1887)
Mussorgsky
(1839-1881)
Rimsky-
Korsakov
(1844-1908)

Liszt
(1811-1886)
Bartók
(1881-1945)
Kodály
(1882-1967)

More about Romantic composers

Composers did not make money unless the public liked their music.

Romantic composers made a living from concerts and from publishing their music. They were not employed by patrons so they had more freedom to experiment. As a result, there is a lot of variety in Romantic music.

Tchaikovsky (1840-1893) was the first Russian composer to be famous outside Russia. He wrote music for ballets* such as *The Sleeping Beauty*, *Swan Lake* and *The Nutcracker*.

Beethoven dedicated his *Eroica Symphony* to Napoleon. But when Napoleon made himself Emperor, Beethoven scratched out the dedication.

Some of Liszt's music was so difficult that only he could play it.

Chopin and Liszt were virtuoso pianists as well as composers.

Beethoven (1770-1827) was the first Romantic composer. He adapted Classical forms to express powerful emotions.

Literature inspired much of Schumann's music.

Romantic music to listen to

Brahms: *Hungarian Dances*.
Borodin: *Polovtsian Dances* from *Prince Igor* Act II.
Chopin: *Polonaises* and *Mazurkas* (Polish dances).
Dvořák: *Slavonic Dances*.
Falla: *Three-cornered Hat* (*El sombrero de tres picos*): ballet suites 1 and 2.
Grieg: *Peer Gynt*.
Liszt: *Hungarian Rhapsodies*.
Schumann: *Manfred* (a setting of the poem by Byron). *Kreisleriana* (piano music inspired by a character called Kreisler invented by the German author Hoffman.)
Sibelius: *Finlandia*.
Smetana: *Ma Vlast* (*My Country*). (This consists of six symphonic poems.)

There are further examples of music to listen to elsewhere on these two pages.

*There is more about ballet music on pages 42-43.

25

TWENTIETH CENTURY MUSIC

In the early 20th century, it was fashionable to experiment with music. You might find some of the results difficult to understand at first.

There were two main trends. One reacted against the emotional, exaggerated quality of Romantic music. The other explored new ways of using key* and harmony.

Experimenting with key

The relationship of music to a key* is called tonality. It means that the music consists of notes from a certain scale*.

Debussy (1862-1918) used a whole-tone scale*, such as the one on the right.

Since the Renaissance, most music had been in major or minor keys. Some 20th century composers made up scales with different rules for which notes were included. This is why some modern music sounds unusual.

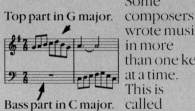

Top part in G major.

Bass part in C major.

Petrushka

Some composers wrote music in more than one key at a time. This is called bitonal music.

Music in more than two keys is called polytonal. Music not written in any key is called atonal.

Parts of Stravinsky's music for the ballet *Petrushka* are bitonal. This helps to describe Petrushka who is a half-human puppet.

The Late Romantics

Around the turn of the century, some composers still expressed Romantic themes but they also began to experiment with tonality. They were called the Late Romantics.

Romantic themes: Emotions Tragedies Stories

Modern tonality: New chord harmonies. Frequent changes or absence of key.

Mahler (1860-1911) was an unhappy man. He expressed his sense of tragedy in his symphonies. He wrote in major or minor keys but he used new, strange-sounding harmonies.

The Impressionists

Realistic art shows all the detail.

Impressionist musicians tried to conjure up sensations through music. They were named after the Impressionist movement in art. Rather than paint realistically,

Impressionist artists tried to convey the impact of a scene using highlights, shadows and splashes of colour.

Serial music

There are 12 different black or white notes in a chromatic scale on a keyboard.

Notes in a chromatic scale are a semitone apart.

In the early 20th century, Schoenberg and his pupils Berg and Webern invented a new style of music. It was based on the chromatic scale*. It was called serial or 12-note music.

Twentieth Century Nationalism

Some Nationalist composers used modern tonality.

Janáček	Czechoslovakia
Bartók and Kodály	Hungary and Rumania
Vaughan Williams and Holst	England

Janáček wrote music based on folk tunes. He built speech rhythms and patterns into his music.

Impressionist art conveys the atmosphere of a scene.

Some Impressionist composers: Debussy Ravel

Note row:

Note row played backwards:

Note row split between two instruments:

Lengths of notes altered:

The composer makes a pattern of notes using each note in the chromatic scale once. The pattern is called a note row, or tone row. The row is then repeated in various ways.

*Keys, scales, tones and semitones are explained on page 19.

Neo-classical music

Classical forms:
Sonata
Concerto
Symphony

Modern features:
New harmonies and tonality.

Neo-Classical composers:
Stravinsky (he also composed serial music – see previous page).
Prokofiev (he was also a Russian Nationalist composer).

"Neo" means new or modernized. Some composers rejected the Romantic style. They combined modern instrumental groups and harmonies with Classical forms.

Everyday music

The Threepenny Opera by Kurt Weill has simple but unusual tunes.

Some 1920s German composers felt that musical experiment was too much for most people. They composed music that more people could enjoy. It was called *Gebrauchsmusik* (utility music).

Minimal or process music

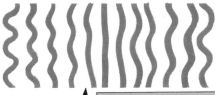

The phrase changes as it is repeated.

Minimal composers:
Philip Glass
Terry Riley
Steve Reich

In the 1960s, a group of North American composers invented minimal music. It consists of repeated phrases which slowly change. It is easier to listen to than some experimental music.

Aleatoric music

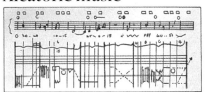

Conventional staffs and symbols may be too precise for aleatoric music. Composers invent new ways to write down, such as this.

Aleatoric music has a chance element, in reaction to music that is totally planned. For instance, it may have phrases that can be played in any order.

John Cage began composing aleatoric music in the 1940s. In some pieces, he puts objects into a piano. This makes its tone and pitch unpredictable.

Musique concrète

Composers:
Schaeffer
Henry

Some 1950s French musicians exploited new sound recording technology. They rearranged sounds on tape, changing the speed or playing them backwards to make musical patterns. This is called *musique concrète*.

Electronic music

Musique concrète: natural sounds manipulated on tape.

Natural sounds altered electronically using samplers*.

Electronic music: electronic sounds produced on a synthesizer.

Electronic sounds created which imitate natural sounds.

In the 1950s, composers such as Stockhausen began to use early synthesizers* to produce electronic music. In the late 1950s, these methods merged with those of *musique concrète*.

Music to listen to

Late Romantic music
Mahler: *Symphony No. 5*.
Richard Strauss: *Also Sprach Zarathustra*.

Twentieth Century Nationalists
Janáček: *The Cunning Little Vixen* (opera).
Bartók: *Rumanian Folk Dances*.
Vaughan Williams: *London Symphony*.

Impressionist music
Debussy: *La Mer*.
Ravel: *Bolero*.

Serial music
Schoenberg: *Five Orchestral Pieces*.

Neo-Classical music
Prokofiev: *Classical Symphony*.
Stravinsky: *Petrushka*.

Gebrauchsmusik
Weill: *The Threepenny Opera*.

Minimal music
Oldfield: *Tubular Bells*.
Reich: *Drumming*.

Aleatoric music
Cage: *Williams Mix*.
Boulez: *Third Piano Sonata*.

Musique concrète
Schaeffer and Henry: *Symphony pour un homme seul*.

Electronic music
Stockhausen: *Mantra*.

*You can read about synthezisers and the other equipment used to make electronic music nowadays on page 29.   27

THE SCIENCE OF SOUND

The difference between music and noise is that musical sounds are organized into patterns and have pitch and rhythm. Noise consists of random, disorganized sounds.

Sounds are made and travel in the same way whether they are musical sounds or noise. Knowing how this happens will help you to understand how musical instruments work.

How sound travels

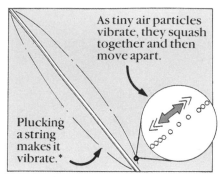

As tiny air particles vibrate, they squash together and then move apart.

Plucking a string makes it vibrate.*

A sound is made when something vibrates and makes particles in the air next to it vibrate. The particles pass the vibration from one to another.

Air pressure
(This axis shows how squashed together or far apart the air particles are.)

Time

This distance is the wavelength. A high sound has a high frequency so the wavelength is short.

This distance is the amplitude. This shows the force with which particles vibrate. A loud sound has a big amplitude.

You can describe a sound by showing it on a graph. The shape is called a sound wave. Different types of sound have different shaped sound waves.

The number of times a sound wave vibrates each second is called frequency. This is measured in cycles per second (cps) or Hertz. A high note has a high frequency.

What makes sounds different?

Most sounds contain higher, quieter sounds mixed in. You do not hear them separately but they add to the tone of the sound. They are called harmonics.

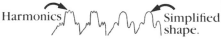

Harmonics Simplified shape.

On a sound wave, harmonics look like little extra waves. They can be smoothed out to get a simpler shape.

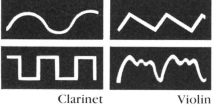

Flute   Trumpet

Clarinet   Violin

Harmonics give an instrument its tone quality. Above are some simplified sound waves made by different instruments.

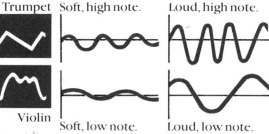

Soft, high note.   Loud, high note.

Soft, low note.   Loud, low note.

The basic shape of a sound wave stays the same when pitch and volume change.

How you hear sound

Your outer ear picks up sound wave vibrations and directs them inside your head.

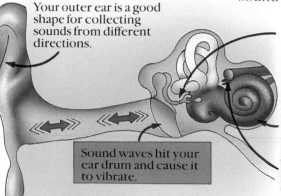

Your outer ear is a good shape for collecting sounds from different directions.

Sound waves hit your ear drum and cause it to vibrate.

Vibrations are passed through your ear to the auditory nerve. This sends a description of the sound vibrations to your brain.

These three bones are called the auditory ossicles. They pass the vibrations along from one to the next.

This tube is called the cochlea. The third auditory ossicle vibrates against it. Vibrations are transmitted through the fluid inside it.

The auditory nerve senses vibrations in the cochlea.

Measuring sound

Sound volume is measured in decibels (dB). A decibel rating tells you how much sound is coming from one source. When a volume doubles, the rating goes up by 6dB. A small plane taking off might have a rating of 95dB. A jet might rate 110dB.

Anything over 105dB can damage your hearing, especially if you are exposed to it for long periods.

*On pages 30-31 you can find out more about how musical instruments make sounds.

ELECTRONIC INSTRUMENTS

Many bands use keyboard synthesizers and drum machines. You can buy cheap versions of synthesizers, called portable keyboards.

Electronic instruments like these contain computer chips, called synthesizer chips. They can store and reproduce sound waves.

How a chip stores a sound wave

A synthesizer chip stores a description of a sound wave in the form of a stream of numbers. These numbers consist of the height of the wave measured at regular intervals. This method of storing sounds is called digitization.

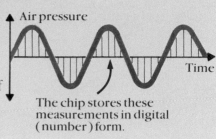

The chip stores these measurements in digital (number) form.

Keyboard synthesizers

A keyboard synthesizer stores different sound waves in digital form. The sounds range from imitations of instruments to buzzes and whistles. They are called pre-set sounds. You select one by pushing the relevant button on the keyboard.

The keyboard changes the pitch of a sound by altering the wave's frequency.

You can link electronic instruments and control them from one place. You need the circuitry called a Musical Instrument Digital Interface (MIDI). This adjusts signals from one device so that another can understand them.

Some expensive synthesizers let you create new sounds. They store several basic wave shapes in digital form. You can mix the shapes and add or remove harmonics to make new shapes.

MIDI circuitry built into a keyboard allows the keyboard player to control a drum machine as well.

Drum or rhythm machines are used in over three quarters of rock music recordings.

Some synthesizers contain a sequencer. This can digitize a tune played on the keyboard. It can replay the tune at any speed or pitch. You can play another tune at the same time.

Drum machines

Drum or rhythm machines store pre-set percussion sounds, such as cymbals, drums or maracas. You choose a sound and play rhythms by tapping on the pads.

You tap on these pads to produce your own rhythm.

If you like, you can record the rhythm. The machine replays it automatically, leaving you free to play another instrument.

The machine also stores pre-set rhythms. You press a button to choose one and start it off.

Playing with sounds

FOOW   WOOF   WOOF

WOOF

Composers of electronic music (see page 27) use sequencers, samplers and synthesizers.

A sampler keyboard can digitize and store live sounds. Once stored, you can play tunes with the sound. You can alter the wave, too; for instance, you can turn it back to front, alter its length or make it echo.

HOW INSTRUMENTS WORK

Similar instruments can be found all over the world. This is because there are only a few ways to make musical sounds. All instruments work by making air particles vibrate (see page 28). They belong to different families depending on how they do this. The families are called percussion, strings, wind, electric and electronic instruments. You can see how they work below.

There is a chart of instrumental families on pages 54-55.

Percussion

You need to hit a percussion instrument to make it vibrate.

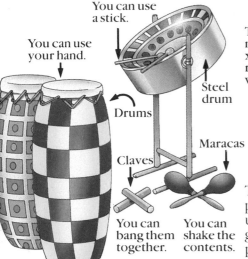

You can use your hand.

You can use a stick.

Steel drum

Drums

Claves

You can bang them together.

Maracas

You can shake the contents.

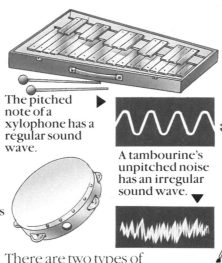

The pitched note of a xylophone has a regular sound wave.

A tambourine's unpitched noise has an irregular sound wave. ▶

There are two types of percussion – pitched and unpitched. Pitched percussion gives a musical note. Unpitched percussion produces noise.

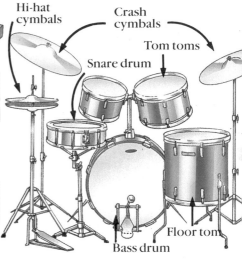

Hi-hat cymbals

Crash cymbals

Tom toms

Snare drum

Floor tom

Bass drum

A drum kit is made up of percussion instruments.

Stringed instruments

You pluck, hit or bow a string on a stringed instrument to make it vibrate. The thicker, longer or looser the string, the lower the sound it makes.

Violin

Double bass

A large frame can support long, thick strings. The larger the instrument, the lower the pitch.

Strings may be made of gut, nylon or metal.

You pluck the strings on a zither.

A vibrating string makes air inside the instrument's body, or soundbox, vibrate. This causes the whole instrument to vibrate. This amplifies the sound and is called resonance.

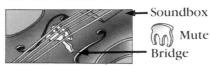

Soundbox

Mute

Bridge

Violin strings are stretched over a piece of wood called a bridge. This carries vibrations from the strings into the soundbox. You can muffle the sound by fixing a clamp called a mute to the bridge. This cuts down on how much the bridge vibrates.

Vibrations travel into the guitar through the hole as well as via the bridge.

String vibrating in sections.

A string vibrates in sections as well as along its whole length. These smaller vibrations produce quieter, higher notes, or harmonics (see page 28).

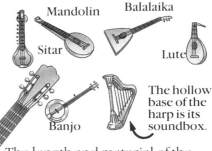

Mandolin

Balalaika

Sitar

Lute

Banjo

The hollow base of the harp is its soundbox.

The length and material of the string determine the harmonics produced. These harmonics and the shape of the soundbox give the instrument its tone.

Wind instruments

Wind instruments work by making a column of air vibrate inside a tube. Covering holes in the tube makes the column longer and the note lower.

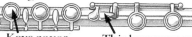

Keys cover large holes.

This lever operates the keys above.

On a large instrument, keys cover holes which are too big for a finger to cover. There are levers to operate keys over holes in awkward places.

Plastic

Silver

There are two types of wind instrument: woodwind and brass. They used to be made from brass or wood but now other materials may be used.

How woodwind instruments work

Some woodwind instruments work by splitting the air flow against an edge.

Another group, called reed instruments, have one or two reeds fixed to a mouthpiece.

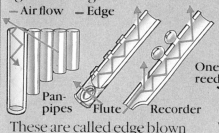

— Air flow   — Edge

Pan-pipes   Flute   Recorder

One reed.

Two reeds.

Two reeds.

Clarinet   Oboe   Bagpipes

These are called edge blown instruments.

When blown, the reeds vibrate and make the air vibrate.

How brass instruments work

To play a brass instrument, you need to make your lips vibrate. You can produce a series of notes from one length of tube by gradually tightening your lips. You can produce further series of notes by pressing valves. These open up further sections of tubing.

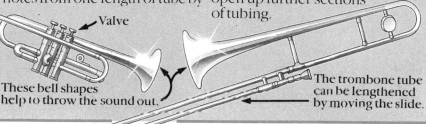

Valve

These bell shapes help to throw the sound out.

The trombone tube can be lengthened by moving the slide.

Keyboard instruments

Keyboard instruments belong to different families depending on how they make sounds.

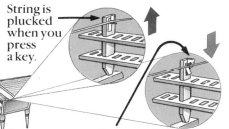

String is plucked when you press a key.

Damper stops string sounding when you release the key.

Damper stops vibrations when you release key.

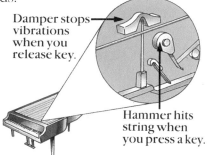

Hammer hits string when you press a key.

The harpsichord has strings which are plucked so this is a stringed instrument.

The piano has strings which are hit so this is both a stringed and a percussion instrument.

An organ has pipes so it is a wind instrument. There is a pipe for each different note.

A synthesizer is an electronic instrument because it makes sounds electronically.*

Electric instruments

An electric instrument uses electricity to amplify sound waves instead of using a soundbox. The picture shows how an electric guitar works. (An electronic instrument uses electricity to make sounds as well as to amplify them.*)

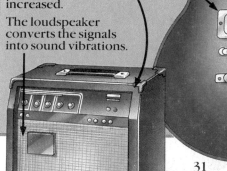

Vibrating air particles round a string are sensed by an electric pick-up.

The pick-up converts the vibrations into electric signals.

These signals are sent to an amplifier where their strength is increased.

The loudspeaker converts the signals into sound vibrations.

*See page 29 for more about electronic instruments.

GROUPS OF INSTRUMENTS

Different instrumental groups provide different musical textures and tones.

The groups shown on these two pages come from all over the world. Each one gives the music of its culture a characteristic sound.

- String section
- Woodwind section
- Brass section
- Percussion section

A symphony orchestra

A symphony orchestra plays the classical music of Europe, North America and Russia. It does not just play symphonies. It may contain over 100 musicians so the orchestra needs a conductor to keep everyone playing together.

The percussion section may include different instruments to those shown, depending on what is needed.

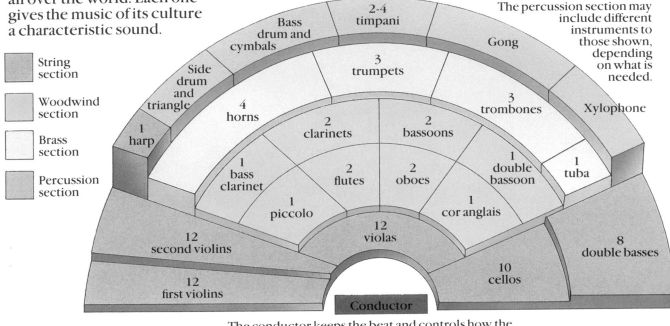

The conductor keeps the beat and controls how the musicians interpret the music (see page 44).

The orchestra is made up of strings, wind and percussion instruments. These give a composer scope to create different effects. The composer does this by choosing certain instruments to play together, balancing and contrasting them.

Some symphonies, especially Romantic ones, need all the instruments. Other classical music only needs a selection.

Playing in tune

When instruments in a group play the same note, the pitch of the notes must match exactly. If they do not, the instruments are said to be out of tune.

Certain things, such as temperature and moisture, cause instruments to go out of tune. This means that the pitch of the notes alters slightly.

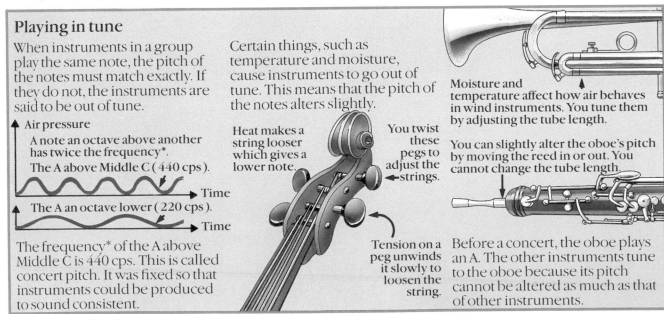

Air pressure

A note an octave above another has twice the frequency*.
The A above Middle C (440 cps).

The A an octave lower (220 cps).

The frequency* of the A above Middle C is 440 cps. This is called concert pitch. It was fixed so that instruments could be produced to sound consistent.

Heat makes a string looser which gives a lower note.

You twist these pegs to adjust the strings.

Tension on a peg unwinds it slowly to loosen the string.

Moisture and temperature affect how air behaves in wind instruments. You tune them by adjusting the tube length.

You can slightly alter the oboe's pitch by moving the reed in or out. You cannot change the tube length.

Before a concert, the oboe plays an A. The other instruments tune to the oboe because its pitch cannot be altered as much as that of other instruments.

A gamelan orchestra

A gamelan is an Indonesian orchestra. The instruments are mostly percussion but there may also be some wind and strings. There can be up to 40 musicians.

Every town or village has its gamelan. The instruments are made locally, so each gamelan has an individual sound.

The music is built around two five-note scales. Musicians learn melodies by heart. They can improvise on the melodies but they must keep to the basic structure to avoid confusion.

South and West African groups

Most South and West African music is based on rhythm. It is very energetic. A lot of it is spontaneous and informal and anyone can join in.

Each player adds a rhythm which fits round existing rhythms. This intricate pattern of rhythms is called polyrhythm. (The Ancient Greek word *poly* means "many".)

Singers might join in with repetitive phrases. They may set up a call and response pattern: someone sings a phrase which is answered by another.

An Indian group

Indian music is not written down. Musicians learn patterns of notes (*ragas*) and rhythms (*talas*) and improvise on them. There are hundreds of *ragas*, each designed for a different season or time of day.

The musicians aim to create a certain mood through the music. They continue for as long as they can sustain the mood or until they have exhausted the scope for improvisation.

The sitar player improvises a tune based on a *raga*.

The tambura player repeats the main note of the *raga* over and over again. This provides a drone, rather like that of a bagpipe.

The tabla player provides the *tala* rhythm.

Music to listen to

Here are some recordings of gamelan music which you could try ordering from a record library. You could also try to locate some records by the African and Indian musicians listed below.

Indonesian gamelan music

Gamelan Femar Pegulingan (Catalogue no. H72046 on the Nonesuch record label). *The Jasmine Isle: Javanese Gamelan Music* (Catalogue no. H72046 on the Nonesuch record label).

West African music

Mustapha Tettey Addy (a drummer from Ghana).
Baaba Maal (Senegal).
King Sunny Adé (Nigeria).
Jali Musa Jawara (Guinea).

South African music

Mahlathini and the Mahotella Queens play a sort of music called *Mbaqanga* which means "township jive".
Makgona Tshole Band.
Ladysmith Black Mambazo.

Indian sitar music

Ustad Vilayat Khan
Ravi Shankar

ALL ABOUT VOICES

People have different ideas about what makes a good voice. Chinese opera singers, for instance, produce a twangy, nasal tone. European singers prefer a fuller sound.

Different voices suit different singing styles. A classical singer needs a strong, clear voice that can be heard at the back of a concert hall. Rock and jazz singers have more varied, natural-sounding voices. Their voices do not need to be so powerful because they use microphones for amplification.

How your voice works

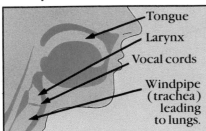

- Tongue
- Larynx
- Vocal cords
- Windpipe (trachea) leading to lungs.

Your voice works like a musical instrument, by making air particles vibrate. This starts in the larynx. Stretched across the larynx are two pieces of skin called the vocal cords.

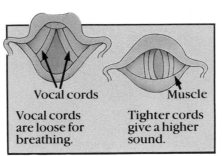

Vocal cords

Muscle

Vocal cords are loose for breathing.

Tighter cords give a higher sound.

When you breathe, the cords loosen to let air past. When you sing or speak, muscles pull the cords tight. The pressure of air squeezing out between them makes them vibrate.

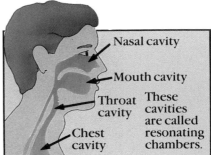

- Nasal cavity
- Mouth cavity
- Throat cavity
- These cavities are called resonating chambers.
- Chest cavity

The vibrating cords make the air in your throat vibrate. Your chest, throat, mouth and nose cavities all start to resonate*. Your breath carries sound waves out of your mouth.

Vocal range

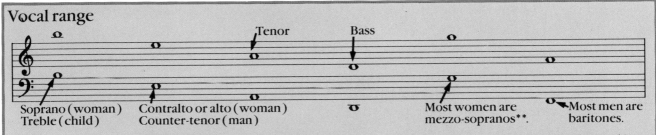

Tenor

Bass

Soprano (woman)
Treble (child)

Contralto or alto (woman)
Counter-tenor (man)

Most women are mezzo-sopranos**.

Most men are baritones.

Everyone finds it a strain to sing above and below certain notes. Each voice has its own limits, called its vocal range. Most voices fall roughly into one of the categories shown above.

Your voice is unique because everyone's vocal cords vary in size. Also, everyone has slightly different-shaped resonating chambers. These alter the shape of the sound waves produced.

Improve your singing

It is easier to sing a note accurately if you imagine it before you sing it. Hearing the note in your head helps your brain to send a clear message to your throat muscles.

Relax so that air can flow uninterrupted from your lungs, out through your throat. Tension can make your throat muscles tighten up, resulting in a strangled sound.

Stand up straight with your feet slightly apart so that you are balanced.

Don't let your head sink. Keep your chin level.

Keep reminding yourself to relax your shoulders. They may tense up as you sing.

Breathe deeply.

Open your throat and feel the air flow freely through it.

Open your mouth wide. It acts as a loudspeaker to send amplified sound waves out of your body.

Aim the sound at the back of the room.

Breathe in deeply and out steadily as you sing. You need breath both to make a sound and to carry it out of your body. If you breathe unsteadily, the notes may wobble or waver out of tune as the air pressure in your larynx alters.

34 *Resonance is explained on page 30.
**"Mezzo" is Italian for "half".

Learning to sing

Training from a skilled teacher can improve your voice in several ways. It teaches you how to use your voice properly and get the best from it.

You can increase your vocal range by at least two notes. Exercises such as singing arpeggios are good for this.

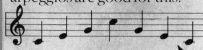

This is an arpeggio. A singer might sing several of these, starting each one a semitone higher than the one before.

Singing scales makes the muscles controlling the vocal cords more flexible. This helps you to pitch notes accurately.

This is a scale.

Breathing exercises such as the one below develop breath control. This helps you to sing long phrases in one breath and to produce contrasts in volume.

Put your hands on your lower ribs, fingertips touching. Breathe in from the bottom of your lungs, and try to make your fingertips move apart.

Relaxation and a better posture can alter the way sound waves resonate inside you. This can improve the tone of your voice. The exercise below helps you to loosen up and stand up straight.

Singing the words

SPOKEN	SUNG
I love you The moon is bright	I lah vyoo The.....moo.....ni .....sbri.....ght

You can only sing clearly and smoothly on vowel sounds. Try to delay sounding consonants for as long as you can.

I'm sorry the dog ate your dinner
I got the Sunday night blues

> This sign means the words are slightly stressed.

A song sounds dull if you give every word the same emphasis. Stress the words as if you were speaking them.

Hold a pen behind your front teeth, flat against your chin. Speak for a minute. When you remove the pen, your pronunciation should be clearer.

When singing softly, you need to exaggerate the shape of your mouth to make the words clear. The exercise above should improve your pronunciation.

Making yourself heard

Singing with other people

Singing in a choir where people sing different notes is called part-singing. The different parts of a choir are usually arranged as shown below.

Tenors	First basses	Second basses
First sopranos	Second sopranos	Altos

This is a close-harmony group. There are usually only one or two singers per part.

It can be difficult to keep to your part when people near you are singing other parts. Try imagining your own part loud in your head as you sing it.

If you hear people whispering, the "s" sounds carry further than any other. Choirs pronounce "s" sounds quietly, to avoid making a loud hiss.

Bob Dylan half sings, half speaks his songs.

Frank Sinatra sang softly and intimately. This is called crooning.

Bruce Springsteen sometimes sings with a tuneful growl.

The way you sing out so that you can be heard is called projection. Classical singers learn to project their voices a long way. The hints on the opposite page should help you project your voice.

Rock, pop and jazz singers use microphones, so they do not need to project their voices as much. They use a variety of vocal styles. For instance, they might growl, half-speak or sing softly.

SONGS AND CHORAL MUSIC

Before printing was invented in the 15th century, people depended on professional musicians to sing new songs to them. After printing was invented, people could buy sheet music to sing and play themselves.

Choral music is for choirs. Most classical choral music is religious because of the custom of singing Christian services. Most choirs were supported by the Church.

Music for the Mass

The main Catholic service is called the Mass. Medieval monks sang the Mass in plainsong. As music developed over the centuries, composers set the Mass to music for church choirs.

A Requiem Mass is a special Mass for the souls of the dead.

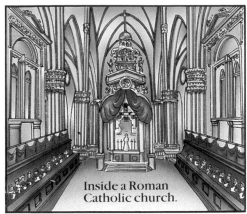

Inside a Roman Catholic church.

The first hymns

Protestant churches were plainer than Catholic churches.

Martin Luther was one of a group of churchmen, called Protestants, who broke away from the Catholic Church in the early 16th century.

Luther wanted everyone to join in the singing in church, not just the choir. He introduced chorales, which were early hymns, into the Protestant service.

Choral symphonies

A choral symphony is written for a choir and symphony orchestra. It balances and contrasts the voices with the instruments.

Oratorios

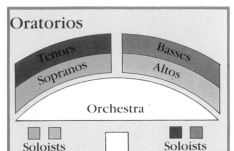

Soloists Conductor Soloists

An oratorio is sung by soloists and a choir accompanied by an orchestra. Oratorios are based on Bible stories. They contain three styles of singing: recitative, chorus and aria. There is no costume or scenery.

Recitative

In recitative, a soloist tells the story. The tune follows the rise and fall and rhythm of speech. A harpsichord or organ plays accompanying chords.

Aria

An aria is a song-like, tuneful solo accompanied by the orchestra. It usually expresses a character's thoughts.

Chorus

A chorus is rather like an aria sung by the choir.

Cantatas

Cantata is Italian for "sung".
Sonata is Italian for "sounded".

A cantata is written for voices accompanied by instruments. Some are small-scale oratorios. Others are non-religious.

Canons and rounds

This is a round.

Second person starts when first person reaches here.

Third person starts when first person reaches here.

A canon is sung or played by a group. Everyone sings or plays the same tune, but a few bars apart. The parts blend together.

The parts may be sung or played at different speeds or even back to front. A round is a simple canon for singers.

Madrigals

Madrigals were popular 16th century songs. They are for two to six voices. Each singer has a different part. There are three main types of madrigal:

A *madrigal proper* is polyphonic*. An *ayre* is a solo accompanied by an instrument or voice. A *ballett* is like an ayre with a cheerful dance rhythm. The chorus often consists of "fa-la-la-la-la".

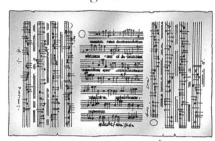

This ayre was printed so that three singers could read from the same page.

Lieder and song cycles

Poem + Words set to music. + Piano accompaniment.

The piano accompaniment creates atmosphere and sets the scene.

Lieder is German for songs. The name is used to describe poems set to music, usually with a piano accompaniment. Most were written in the 19th century.

Schubert (1797-1828) wrote over 600 *Lieder*. He once wrote eight in one day. He also wrote song cycles (groups of songs which tell a story or share a theme).

Speech songs

Schoenberg developed a vocal style that mixes elements from speech and song. It is called *sprechstimme* (speaking voice)

or *sprechgesang* (speech song). The singer follows written music but does not fully sing the notes.

Schoenberg's music for the ballet *Pierrot Lunaire* contains *sprechstimme*.

Elements from speech: Rhythm and tone are similar to speech. The pitch may follow the rise and fall of speech. The voice may slide between notes rather than pitch them separately.

Elements from song: Singing techniques are used for clarity and projection. The composer decides on the rise and fall of pitch.

*Each part is an independent tune.

Music to listen to

A baroque Mass
Charpentier: *Messe de Minuit*.

A Classical Mass
Mozart: *Coronation Mass*.

A modern Mass
Janáček: *Glagolitic Mass*.

Requiem Masses
Fauré: *Requiem*.
Britten: *War Requiem*. This contains poems by Wilfrid Owen, a British poet killed in World War I.

Chorales
Bach: *Wachet Auf!* (*Sleepers awake!*). *Jesu, Joy of Man's Desiring* (from *Cantata 147*).

Choral symphonies
Beethoven: *Symphony No. 9*.
Mahler: *Symphony No. 8*.
Britten: *Spring Symphony*.

Oratorios
Handel: *Messiah*.
Haydn: *The Creation*.
Elgar: *The Dream of Gerontius*.
Tippett: *A Child of Our Time*.

Cantatas
Bach: *The Christmas Oratorio*.
Mendelssohn: *Hymn of Praise*.
Britten: *Cantata Misericordium*.

Madrigals
Some madrigal composers are Morley, Byrd, Tallis, Gibbons and Monteverdi.

Lieder
Schubert: *Der Erlkönig* (*The Erl King*). *Die Forelle* (*The Trout*).
Brahms: *Wiegenlied* (*Lullaby*).
Richard Strauss: *Morgen* (*Morning*).

Song cycles
Schubert: *Die Schöne Müllerin* (*The Maid of the Mill*).
Schumann: *Dichterliebe* (*Poet's Love*).
Berlioz: *Les Nuits d'Eté* (*Summer Nights*).
Britten: *On This Island*.

Sprechstimme
Schoenberg: *Pierrot Lunaire*.
Berio: *Sequenza III*.

OPERA

An opera is a musical play. The words (called the *libretto*) may all be sung, or some may be spoken.

How opera began

Opera began in Italy at the very end of the 16th century. The first operas consisted of recitative* alone. This was an attempt to revive a sort of Ancient Greek drama in which actors may have recited words to music. Operas were performed in private to aristocrats.

Recitative was accompanied by a harpsichord or organ and bass viol, playing a figured bass**.

Monteverdi's operas

Monteverdi (1567-1643), an Italian composer, added arias*, choruses and dances to opera. These made it more fun. He used recitative for conversation or to tell the story. This became the normal pattern for opera. Operas became very popular and many had terrific special effects, using trap doors, trapezes, fire and water.

Opera stars

Successful opera singers became wealthy celebrities. Composers often created roles for certain singers. Singers influenced composers because they could attract audiences. Some would only sing music that flattered their voices. An elaborate aria which shows off a singer's vocal agility is called a *coloratura* aria.

Serious opera

Opera seria is Italian for serious opera. These were 18th century operas in Italian about Ancient Greek gods and heroes. They did not have choruses, so they were cheaper to stage.

It became fashionable to be seen at the opera but audiences did not always listen to the music. It was a social occasion and people talked through the singing. Some even played chess.

Comic opera

Comic opera developed in the early 18th century in reaction to *opera seria*. The music was simpler and the story was usually about ordinary people rather than grand historical figures.

Italian comic opera was called *opera buffa*. In time, the styles of *opera buffa* and *opera seria* merged. For instance, Mozart's *The Marriage of Figaro* (1786), contains different styles of singing.

English comic opera was called ballad opera. Speech replaced recitative. Some songs were based on popular songs. *The Beggar's Opera* (1728) by John Gay is a ballad opera which makes fun of Italian *opera seria*.

German ballad operas are known as *Singspiel* (sing-play).

*Recitative, aria and chorus are explained on page 36.
**You can find out what a figured bass is on page 39.

38

Italian opera in London

Handel (1685-1759)* settled in London and wrote Italian *opera seria*. For a while his operas were popular but people began to prefer ballad opera. Many also liked music with a chorus, so Handel began to write oratorios**.

Wagner's music-dramas

Wagner (1813-1883) created a new style of opera which consisted of music without breaks between aria and recitative. He called the operas music-dramas. He wrote his own libretti so he had control of the effect of the words and music.

French opera

An Italian called Lully (1632-1687) was music director at the French court of Louis XIV. He and his successor Rameau (1683-1764) developed a French opera style. Here are some features:

- The libretto was in French.
- French opera was more stately than dramatic Italian opera.
- The King liked ballet so each opera contained a ballet.
- French operas had elaborate overtures. Italian operas had simpler overtures, called *sinfonias*.

Wagner used musical themes, or *leitmotifs*, to stand for ideas, people or objects. A *leitmotif* may consist of a tune or chord sequence. They are woven into the music at appropriate times.

Ring

Valkyrie (Norse goddess)

Fafnir the Dragon

Sword

ENGLAND

GERMANY

FRANCE

ITALY

Wagner gives these creatures and objects musical themes, or *leitmotifs*, in his operas.

Opéra comique

Opéra comique is 19th century French opera with speech instead of recitative. It is not comic opera; for example, Bizet's *Carmen* (1875) has a sad ending.

Grand opera

Grand opera is serious 19th century opera. It is all set to music. It has a heroic story, a large chorus and magnificent scenery and costume. This scene is from the opera *Aida* by Verdi (1813-1901), an Italian composer.

Wagner based his operas on German and Norse legend. This scene is from *Lohengrin* which is about a medieval German knight.

Modern opera

Britten's *Peter Grimes* is about a fisherman who is a social outcast.

During the 20th century, some composers began to explore people's minds and motives. This was a change from using opera just to tell stories.

Light opera or operetta

This scene is from Offenbach's *Orpheus in the Underworld*.

An operetta is a light-hearted play with songs. The story is usually romantic or makes fun of people. It is high-spirited and often contains dancing.

Musicals

The Phantom of the Opera was one of Andrew Lloyd Webber's many hits.

Musicals grew from operetta. The songs provide atmosphere but the spoken words tell the story. The stories can be light-hearted or serious.

*You can read more about Handel on page 20.
**You can find out about oratorios on page 36.*

Listening to opera

Most operas were written in Italian, French or German. Some companies perform them in English, though. Even so, it can be difficult to follow all the words. If you are going to an opera, try to find a library book which tells you the story of the opera before you go. The programme notes may also help.

Famous opera stars

Here are some famous opera stars from around the world.

Kiri Te Kanawa

Sopranos

Kiri Te Kanawa, New Zealand.

Jessye Norman, America.

Joan Sutherland, Australia.

Grace Bumbry, America.

Grace Bumbry

Mezzo-sopranos

Marilyn Horne, America.

Teresa Berganza, Spain.

Frederica von Stade, America.

Placido Domingo

Tenors

Placido Domingo, Spain.

Luciano Pavarotti, Italy.

José Carreras, Spain.

Thomas Allen

Baritones

Thomas Allen, Great Britain.

Sherrill Milnes, America.

Samuel Ramey, America.

Willard White

Basses

Willard White, Great Britain.

Robert Lloyd, Great Britain.

John Tomlinson, Great Britain.

Famous opera houses

Sydney Opera House, Australia, opened in 1973.

La Scala, Milan, Italy, built in 1778.

The Royal Opera House, London, England.

This was first built in 1732 and last rebuilt in 1858.

The Metropolitan, New York, USA, built in 1966.

The Kirov Theatre, Leningrad, Russia, built in 1860.

The Festspielhaus, Bayreuth, West Germany, built by Wagner for his operas in 1876.

Opera to listen to

Early opera
Monteverdi: *Orpheus, The Coronation of Poppaea.*

Opera seria
Mozart: *Idomeneo.*

Opera buffa
Rossini: *The Barber of Seville.*
Mozart: *The Marriage of Figaro, Don Giovanni.*

Ballad opera
Gay: *The Beggar's Opera.*

Singspiel
Mozart: *The Magic Flute.*

Opéra comique
Bizet: *Carmen.*
Gounod: *Faust.*

Music drama
Wagner: *The Ring of the Nibelung* (a cycle of four operas, called *Rhinegold, The Valkyrie, Siegfried* and *The Twilight of the Gods*). *The Flying Dutchman, Lohengrin.*

Grand opera
Rossini: *William Tell.*
Verdi: *Aida, La Traviata, Rigoletto.*
Puccini: *La Bohème, Madame Butterfly, Tosca.*

Modern opera
Britten: *Peter Grimes.*
Tippett: *Midsummer Marriage.*
Josephs: *Rebecca.*

Operetta
Offenbach: *Orpheus in the Underworld.*
Johann Strauss: *Die Fledermaus.*
Gilbert and Sullivan: listen to any of their operettas.

Musicals
Gershwin: *Porgy and Bess.*
Bernstein: *West Side Story.*
Rodgers and Hammerstein: *Oklahoma, South Pacific.*
Bart: *Oliver!*
Lloyd Webber: *Evita, Phantom of the Opera, Cats, Aspects of Love.*

FILM AND BACKGROUND MUSIC

Music is rather like a wordless language to which people respond emotionally. Because of this, it helps create an atmosphere for a film or TV programme. It is used to put the audience in a certain mood.

Music can make people relax. This is why some public places have background music. Instead of finding it soothing, though, some people are irritated by it because it is often bland and predictable.

Film music

A film might have a theme tune at the beginning or end. Music during the film (incidental music) might contain variations on the theme. This helps to give the film its own identity.

The theme tune sets the mood for the start of the film.

Dramatic incidental music helps provide atmosphere.

Cheerful music accompanies a happy ending.

Cinema sound systems

There are four sets of speakers in a cinema. (A set may consist of more than one speaker.) Sound can come from anywhere, depending on which set it is played through. This system of reproducing sound is called Dolby Stereo.

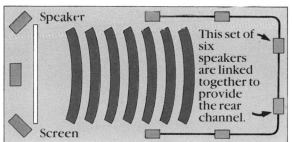

Speaker

This set of six speakers are linked together to provide the rear channel.

Screen

Speech comes from the front, near the actors on the screen.

Crowd noise comes from all around you, from all the speakers.

In a horror movie, sudden noises may come from behind.

Composing film music

The film director chooses a composer to write the music for a film. They discuss what sort of music would suit the film and which scenes will have music. The composer needs to time the music so that it fits the action on the screen.

One frame from a film.

`01.23.56.12`

A film has 24 frames per second. This is the twelfth frame in this second of the film.

The composer is given an early version of the film on video. Each frame has a number showing hours, minutes, seconds and frame number. This helps the composer work out how long a scene is so that he or she can time the music to fit it.

Music for silent movies

Films did not have soundtracks until the 1930s. Before then, each cinema employed a pianist to improvise an accompaniment to the film. There were common themes for love, fear and so on.

Background music

Background music is meant to relax you so that you browse around and buy more.

Background music is played because some people think that silence can be disturbing. Most background music consists of instrumental versions of well-known songs, or popular classical pieces. These are arranged so that nothing stands out or demands attention. The tune used most often for background music is the Beatles' *Yesterday*.

Here are some places where background music might be played.
Shopping malls
Lifts
Waiting rooms
Cafes
Railway stations
Sports centres

DANCE AND BALLET MUSIC

Dancing provides a way for people to join in musical entertainment. Disco music, for instance, is supposed to make you want to get up and dance.

Some kinds of dancing, such as ballet, have become so highly developed that only trained dancers can perform them. People enjoy watching the skill and grace with which the dancers perform the movements.

In all types of dance, music provides a framework for the movements.

Dancing is a sociable activity. This is why a lot of folk and popular music is dance music.

Sri Lankan temple dancers.

Some forms of worship include dance. The medieval Christians, though, associated dance with fun and frivolity and had nothing to do with it.

Japanese Noh drama is skilled entertainment. It is a slow dance-like mime to music.

The story of ballet

 First (*en première*)   Second (*en seconde*)

The five basic positions of the feet in ballet.

Third (*en troisième*) Fourth (*en quatrième*) Fifth (*en cinquante*)

Marie Taglioni (1804-1884) was the first to dance on the tips of her toes (*en pointe*).

During the 15th and 16th centuries, there was a type of court entertainment consisting of song and dance. The origins of ballet go back to this.

Louis XIV ruled France from 1643-1715. He founded the first ballet school. Ballet steps have French names because many of them were established there.

By the 19th century, ballet had developed into a style with a strict technique. This style is called classical ballet. These ballets usually tell a story.

Ghosts of maidens who died before their weddings appear in *Giselle*.

In the first half of the 19th century, ballets had Romantic* themes, such as tragic love affairs or supernatural events.

The Prince wakes Princess Aurora in *The Sleeping Beauty*.

Ballets of the second half of the 19th century show classical ballet at its grandest. They show off the dancers' skill.

This is from the Modern ballet called *The Four Temperaments*.

20th century Modern ballets may explore emotions rather than tell stories. The movements are based on classical techniques.

Contemporary dance

Some 20th century dancers reacted against the discipline of classical ballet. They explored less restricted ways of moving and responding to music. The resulting styles are called contemporary dance.

Classical ballerinas dance on points in order to look weightless and fragile. The men are meant to look strong and heroic.

Contemporary dancers may dance in bare feet and use their weight for effect. Men's and women's roles are less stereotyped.

Making a dance or ballet

The choreographer works on the movements with the dancers.

Some ballets have music specially composed for them. Others are inspired by an existing piece of music. The person who has the idea for a ballet and creates the movements is called a choreographer.

Music and mood

Music contributes to the mood of a ballet or dance. The rhythm, tune, and choice of instruments all play a part.

Changes in mood and music usually accompany a change of scene. The contrast helps to keep the audience interested.

Stravinsky's music for *The Rite of Spring* is meant to sound barbaric. The ballet is about a ritual in which a girl is chosen as a sacrifice. She has to dance herself to death.

Orchestra pit in front of stage.

Music for a classical ballet is usually performed live by an orchestra. Music for a contemporary dance may be live or it may be on tape.

Some contemporary dances use the rhythms of speech instead of music. Some are performed in silence. The dancers carry the rhythms of the dance in their minds and bodies.

Ballet music to listen to

You may not be able to find complete recordings of all these ballets. Instead, you might come across compilation albums which contain the most popular excerpts.

Romantic ballet music
Adam: *Giselle*.
Scheitzhoeffner: *La Sylphide*.

Classical ballet music (second half of the 19th century)
Tchaikovsky: *Swan Lake*, *The Sleeping Beauty*, *The Nutcracker*.
Delibes: *Coppélia*.

Late classical ballet music
Chopin: *Les Sylphides* (1909).
Debussy: *L'Après-Midi d'un Faune* (1912).
Stravinsky: *The Firebird* (1910), *The Rite of Spring* (1913).

Modern ballets
Falla: *The Three-Cornered Hat* (1919).
Prokofiev: *Romeo and Juliet* (1935).
Franck: *Symphonic Variations* (1946).
Ravel: *Daphnis and Chloë* (1910).
Joplin: *Elite Syncopations* (1974).

American ballet music
Copland: *Billy the Kid* (1938), *Rodeo* (1942), *Appalachian Spring* (1944).

COMPOSING AND PERFORMING

Composing and performing both require a mixture of skill and inspiration. You need technical skill to help you to put your ideas across in the music. Inspiration will help you to bring life and feeling to the piece.

A conductor needs inspiration, as well as the ability to control a large number of musicians.

How composers work

Many composers explore tunes and harmonies and develop them at an instrument or with others during a jam session.

Beethoven's manuscripts were untidy.

Most composers produce a first version of the music and then alter, improve and refine it.

One of Mozart's manuscripts.

Mozart could compose long orchestral works in his head and then write them out. They would need no alteration.

A composer needs inspiration, or a starting point. This might come from anywhere.

How conducting developed

An orchestra is like a huge instrument which the conductor plays. The smaller the group of instruments, the less need there is for a conductor to keep them together.

In the 18th century, when orchestras were small, the harpsichord player or chief violinist would often direct the music. As orchestras grew in size in the 19th century, the custom of conducting with a baton became established.

A conductor's job

A conductor is in control of an orchestra and decides how they should play a piece of music.

He or she needs a thorough knowledge of the capabilities and limitations of each instrument.

The conductor needs to be able to hear if any instrument is out of tune.

The conductor must ensure that the instruments are all playing in time with each other.

The conductor checks the sound balance. No instrument should stand out unless it is meant to.

Conducting technique

The conductor uses a stick or baton to indicate the number of beats in the bar and the *tempo* (speed).

The conductor uses the other hand to express how the music should be played and to give cues. These tell instruments exactly when to start.

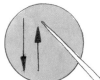
2 beats in a bar.

3 beats in a bar.

4 beats in a bar.

Quiet

Loud

Giving a cue.

Playing to an audience

Playing in public can be nerve-racking. Once you have started playing, though, concentration on the music usually replaces fear. Here are some hints:

- Appear confident on the stage. Don't shuffle on.

- Play with conviction and the audience are more likely to relax and enjoy themselves.

- If you make a mistake, don't go back to correct it.

- The better you know the piece, the more confident you will be.

- If there is a conductor, keep looking at him or her. Don't bury your head in the music.

- If you are part of a group, listen to the others so that you can adjust your playing to fit in with them.

Acoustics

Sound behaves in different ways depending on the volume, shape and sound absorbent qualities of a building. The way sound behaves is called acoustics.

Sound waves bounce off walls and ceilings. Reflected sound waves reach you after direct ones. This lengthens the sound and is called reverberation.

People's bodies absorb sound. Tipped-up seats are designed to absorb the same amount of sound as a body so that acoustics in a full or empty hall are similar.

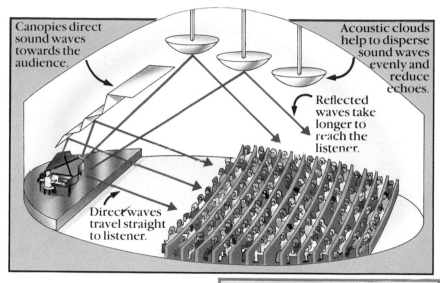

Canopies direct sound waves towards the audience.

Acoustic clouds help to disperse sound waves evenly and reduce echoes.

Reflected waves take longer to reach the listener.

Direct waves travel straight to listener.

Reverberation times

The length of time it takes for a sound to die away is called its reverberation time. If the reverberation time is very short, the music sounds dead.

If you sing outside, your voice sounds thin and small. This is because the sound waves have nothing to reverberate against and they die away quickly.

If the reverberation time is too long, it becomes difficult to distinguish between different strands of music. They blend into one another.

Sound waves bounce between surfaces, giving an echoey effect.

A stone church may have a reverberation time of up to seven seconds. Most concert halls have a reverberation time of one or two seconds.

Singing in the bath

Sound waves get weaker the further they travel. The energy of the wave is used up in moving air particles.* In a small room, sound waves bounce back off the walls before they have travelled far. You hear them all about the same time. This makes your voice sound louder than in a large room.

*See page 28 for more about how sound travels.

SOUND REPRODUCTION

There are three ways to store sound: on tape, record or compact disc.

Cassette tapes are easy to carry about and you can use them in personal stereos. They give about the same sound quality as records but they wear out faster. Compact discs give the best quality and last longest but they are the most expensive.

Recording on tape

Music is first recorded on tape, even if it is going to end up on record or disc.

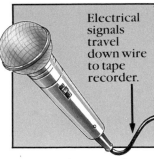

Electrical signals travel down wire to tape recorder.

Record head.   Tape

A microphone picks up sound vibrations in the air and converts them into an electric current of varying strength, or voltage.

The electrical signals are fed into a tape recorder. The record head converts them into magnetic forces of varying strength.

The record head lays down magnetic patterns on the surface of the tape.

Playing a cassette

The playback head in a cassette player translates the magnetic pattern on a tape into a series of voltages. These are strengthend (amplified) and then changed into sound by a loudspeaker.

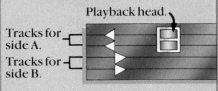

Playback head.

Tracks for side A.
Tracks for side B.

Cassette tape is divided into four tracks. The playback head sits over two at a time. Each pair provides a stereo sound (see next page). When you turn the tape over, the playback head reads the other two tracks.

Analogue recording

An analogue, or non-digital, tape recorder stores signals from the microphone as a continuously varying magnetic pattern.

Digital recording

A digital tape recorder measures the voltage from the microphone up to 50,000 times per second. It stores each measurement as a binary number, represented by on and off signals.*

Digital recording is more accurate than analogue. It is easier to tell the difference between an on or off signal than to detect tiny variations in a voltage.

Multitrack recording

Professional recording studios use tape recorders with up to 32 record heads. Each head receives signals from one or more microphones and records a separate track on the tape. This is called multitracking.

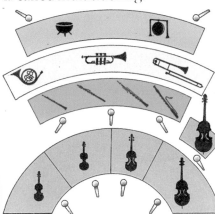

This is how microphones might be set up for multitrack recording of an orchestra in a concert hall.

In a studio, the tracks may be recorded one at a time. If a mistake is made, the track can be re-recorded.

This singer can hear previously-recorded tracks through headphones.

The producer and sound engineer listen to each track and adjust its tone or volume. They also adjust the balance of sound between the tracks. They mix the tracks at a mixing desk and record them on to a master tape.

*This is digitization. There is more about it on page 9.

Portable recording studios

A four-track tape recorder, or portable studio, costs about as much as two compact disc players. It is useful for demo tapes and trying ideas out.

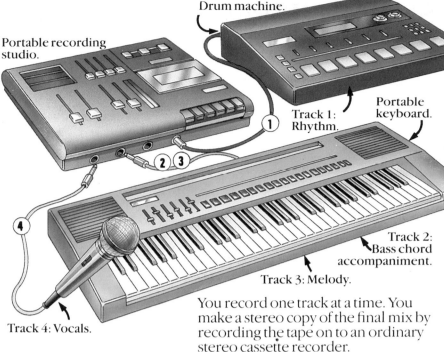

Drum machine.

Portable recording studio.

Track 1: Rhythm.

Portable keyboard.

① ② ③

④

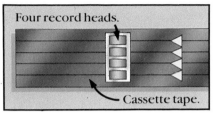

Four record heads.

Cassette tape.

A portable studio uses ordinary cassette tape. Instead of two record heads as on a stereo cassette recorder, there are four record heads, one for each track. You cannot turn the tape over as all the tracks are used up by the four record heads.

Track 4: Vocals.

Track 2: Bass chord accompaniment.

Track 3: Melody.

You record one track at a time. You make a stereo copy of the final mix by recording the tape on to an ordinary stereo cassette recorder.

Making a record

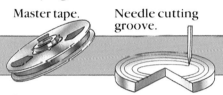

Master tape.

Needle cutting groove.

Stamper for each side of record.

Finished record.

Stylus vibrating against outer wall gives right-hand stereo signal.

Vibrations against inner wall give left-hand stereo signal.

Magnetic patterns on a tape are converted into voltages. These control a needle which carves a groove in a circular sheet of

aluminium covered with plastic. Metal moulds, or stampers, are made from this. They are used to make copies in vinyl.

When you play a record, the irregularities in the groove make the stylus vibrate. These vibrations are converted into voltages, amplified and sent to the loudspeaker.

Stereo sound

A stereo system sends out a different mix of sounds from each speaker. This gives the impression of musicians in different positions. To get the best from your stereo, set up the speakers as below.

The speakers should be at the same level as your ears.

Put the speakers near but not against the wall.

Sit about the same distance away from each one.

How a compact disc works

A compact disc, or CD, stores music in digital form. The disc is made of aluminium coated with a transparent, protective vinyl layer. The aluminium surface contains millions of tiny pits.

Inside a CD player, a laser beam scans the disc's surface. It senses where the pits are and the CD player converts the information into a series of binary numbers. They are the measurements of the sound waves which make up the music.

A CD is tough. There is no contact between the laser beam and the disc so they do not wear each other out. The beam is focussed on the aluminium surface so it travels through scratches on the vinyl coating.

Pits on surface of disc.

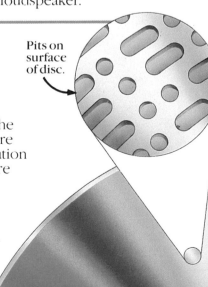

HOW TO READ MUSIC

The next six pages tell you how music is written down. Look at pages 18-19 if you need to be reminded of the basics. There is a lot to remember so you will need practice before you can read music quickly and accurately, or write your own tunes down.

Note lengths

The length of a sound is shown by a symbol. The chart shows all the different symbols and the lengths of time they stand for. The alternative names in brackets may help you to remember how long the notes are. For instance, a quarter note is a quarter of a whole note.

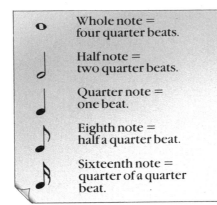

Whole note =
four quarter beats.

Half note =
two quarter beats.

Quarter note =
one beat.

Eighth note =
half a quarter beat.

Sixteenth note =
quarter of a quarter beat.

A time signature where each beat is worth an eighth, quarter or half note is known as a simple time signature. (See the examples under **Beats and bars** on the left.) Here are the most common simple time signatures.

Bars divided into half beats.	Bars divided into quarter beats.	Bars divided into eighth beats.
2 3 4 / 2 2 2	2 3 4 / 4 4 4	2 3 4 / 8 8 8

Compound time signatures

In some time signatures, called compound time signatures, a bar is divided into beats which last for the length of a dotted note.

The most common compound time signature is $\frac{6}{8}$ time. It has two beats in each bar. Each beat is the length of a dotted quarter (or three eighths).

I will eat yours and then I'll eat mine.

Some other compound time signatures are:

There are two beats, each worth a dotted half (or three quarters) in a bar.

There are three beats, each worth a dotted quarter (or three eighths) in a bar.

Beats and bars

Most rhythms are arranged around groups of steady beats, called bars. There are usually two, three or four beats in a bar. The first beat in each bar is usually the strongest.

The time signature at the beginning of a line of music tells you how many beats there are in each bar and what sort of beats they are. Try saying the phrases below to hear the rhythms.

This top number tells you that there are four beats in each bar.

Bar lines separate the bars.

There is always a double bar line at the end of a piece of music.

STAND up straight and PULL your socks up.

This tells you that the beats are quarter notes.

SEA-weed ri-SOT-to and JELLy-fish SANDwiches

Three eighth note beats in a bar.

Two half note beats in a bar.

Two quarter notes last as long as one half note.

SING ve-ry LOUD-ly and FRIGHTen the NEIGHbours

Dotted notes

A dot after a note makes it half as long again. Below you can see how long each kind of dotted note lasts.

Dotted whole note: four + two = six quarter beats.

Dotted half note: two + one = three quarter beats.

Dotted quarter note: one and a half quarter beats (three eighth beats).

Dotted eighth note: one and a half eighth beats (three sixteenth beats).

Silences in the music: rests

A silence in music is called a rest. Rest symbols show the length of the silence. Below is a chart of rest symbols.

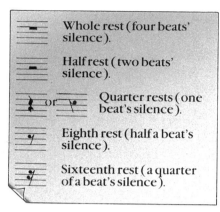

A bar of music must contain the full number of beats, even if some of those beats are silent. Here are two examples:

The notes and rests in each bar add up to four beats.

A quarter rest lasts for one beat.

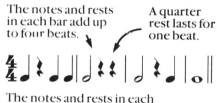

The notes and rests in each bar add up to three beats.

Making music easier to read

Groups of eighth notes and shorter notes written in the music are usually joined together to make it easier to read. In simple time, the notes are joined together to make up the value of a quarter note beat.

Two eighths.

Four sixteenths.

Two sixteenths and one eighth.

Dotted eighth and one sixteenth.

In simple time, a separate rest is normally used for each beat of silence in the music.

Two quarter rests.

Half rest.

In compound time, you can use a dotted rest or two rests for a silent beat (one and a half quarter notes).

or

A bar's rest is represented by a whole rest, whatever the time signature.

In compound time, the beat consists of a dotted note. Eighth and sixteenth notes are joined together to make up the value of the dotted note.

You may come across the following groupings in $\frac{6}{8}$ time. Each group makes up the length of a dotted quarter note.

Three eighths.

A dotted eighth, a sixteenth and an eighth.

Two sixteenths and two eighths.

Tied notes

You can make a note longer by joining it to another with a little curved line. You play the first note but hold it for the length of the two notes added together.

A whole note tied to a half note gives six beats.

Tied notes can cross a bar line:

These tied quarters last for two beats.

Triplets

A composer might want to fit three notes into the space of one quarter note beat. There is no note symbol standing for a third of a quarter note. Instead, the pattern below represents three notes of equal length, taking up one quarter note beat. This pattern is called a triplet.

Triplet

Starting in the middle of a bar

Not all rhythms start on the first beat of a bar. If there is an incomplete bar at the beginning of the music, the missing beats are used up at the end. Here are some examples.

I'm go-ing to see the boss.

One beat at the beginning.

Two beats at the end.

Don't you ev-er tell a soul.

Two beats at the beginning.

Two beats at the end.

Major scales

All major scales have the same pattern of tones and semitones within them (see page 19.)

T = tone   S = semitone

To keep this pattern, every major scale except C major has to use one or more black notes on the keyboard instead of white ones.

A black note which replaces the note below it is called a sharp. The scale of D major contains two sharps:

Sharp sign. This tells you to play the note a semitone above F.

A note which replaces the note above it is called a flat. The scale of F major contains one flat:

Flat sign. This tells you to play the note a semitone below B.

Minor scales

There are two forms of minor scale. The harmonic minor contains an interval of three semitones which is not easy to sing. The melodic minor does not contain this interval. Here is the pattern of the harmonic minor form of scale.

T = tone   S = semitone
T½ = 1½ tones (three semitones).

Below is the scale of A harmonic minor.

The melodic minor is the same as the harmonic scale except that the sixth note is raised a semitone on the way up the scale. It also has a different pattern going down the scale, as shown below.

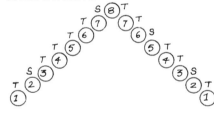

minor shown on a keyboard and written out on a staff.

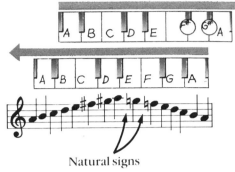

Natural signs

A natural sign changes a note back from a sharp or flat into the white note just above or below it.

Relative scales

The last three notes of a major scale form the first three notes of a minor scale. For instance, the last three notes of the scale of C major are the same as the first three notes of A minor. A minor is known as the relative minor scale of C major. C major is A minor's relative major.

C major

A harmonic minor.

Keys and key signatures

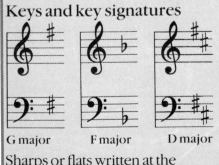

G major   F major   D major

Sharps or flats written at the beginning of the staff show that the music is written in the key that contains those sharps or flats. The signs are called the key signature.

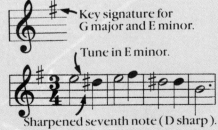

Key signature for G major and E minor.

Tune in E minor.

Sharpened seventh note (D sharp).

A minor scale has the same key signature as its relative major. The seventh note in a minor scale needs a sharp sign written in front of it whenever it occurs in the music.

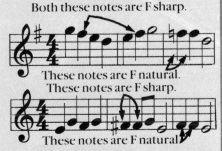

Both these notes are F sharp.

These notes are F natural.
These notes are F sharp.

These notes are F natural.

The key signature affects the whole piece. Naturals, sharps and flats elsewhere in the music are called accidentals. These only affect the rest of the bar in which they appear.

Names of notes in a scale

Each note in a scale has a name which describes its position in the scale. These names are used to describe chords based on the notes. The names can also be used to describe how a piece of music changes key. For instance, a sonata might start in C major, called the tonic or home key. It might then change key (modulate) into the dominant key, which is the key of G major.

Tonic (The note from which the scale takes its name.)

Supertonic (The note above the tonic.)

Mediant (Mid-way between the tonic and the dominant.)

Sub-dominant (The same distance below the tonic as the dominant is above it.)

Dominant (The next most important note to the tonic.)

Sub-mediant (Mid-way between the upper tonic and the sub-dominant.)

Leading note (In a tune, this sounds as if it should be followed by the tonic.)

Tonic (An octave above the lower tonic.)

Intervals and harmony

Harmony is made up of a series of chords. The intervals between notes in a chord give the chord its particular sound. Below are the names of some intervals. The names describe the distance between two notes of different pitch. To identify an interval by number, count the lines and spaces between the notes including those on which the notes are written.

Major second (two semitones).

Major third (four semitones).

Perfect fourth (five semitones).

Perfect fifth (seven semitones).

Major sixth (nine semitones).

Major seventh (eleven semitones).

Octave (twelve semitones).

These intervals have a simple, pure sound. This is why they are called perfect.

Minor third

Minor seventh

Diminished fourth

Augmented sixth

Augmented fifth

If a major interval is made smaller by one semitone, it is called a minor interval.

If a minor or perfect interval is made smaller by a semitone, it is a diminished interval.

If a major or perfect interval is increased by a semitone, it becomes an augmented interval.

Names of intervals

In the context of intervals, "minor" means "less". A minor interval is one semitone less than a major interval. A minor scale does not contain all the minor intervals.

Some intervals have two names. For instance, a perfect fourth is the same as an augmented third. The name depends on the number of notes involved when the interval is written on the staff.

Building chords

The simplest three-note chord you can play is called a tonic triad. This consists of the first, third and fifth notes in the scale. It provides a settled, final-sounding ending to a piece of music. You can play it with any of the three notes in the chord at the bottom.

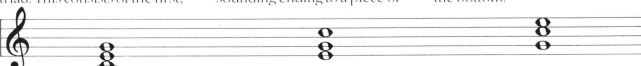

The order first, third, fifth is called the root position.

The order third, fifth, first is called the first inversion.

The order fifth, first, third is called the second inversion.

Chord progressions and resolution

A succession of chords is called a chord progression or harmonic progression. Western harmony is mostly based on chord progressions. This style took over from polyphony during the 17th century (see pages 20-21).

A chord made up of notes that sound good together is called a concord. A chord made up of notes that clash is called a discord.

This shows a concord following a discord.

A discord has an incomplete feel to it, so a chord progression usually ends on a concord. The process of following a discord with a concord is called resolution.

Building triads

You can build triads on every note of a scale. This shows triads built on each note of the scale of C major. They are numbered with Roman numerals to show which note of the scale they are built on. For example, chord V in C major is built on the fifth note of the scale.

A major triad is made up of a major third and a perfect fifth from the lowest note.

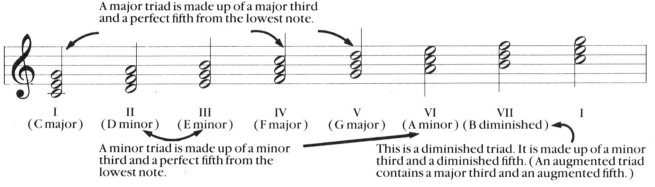

I	II	III	IV	V	VI	VII	I
(C major)	(D minor)	(E minor)	(F major)	(G major)	(A minor)	(B diminished)	

A minor triad is made up of a minor third and a perfect fifth from the lowest note.

This is a diminished triad. It is made up of a minor third and a diminished fifth. (An augmented triad contains a major third and an augmented fifth.)

The names in brackets describe the chords shown. Some of the chords sound bright and cheerful. Others sound sad and wistful.

The cheerful ones are the major tonic triads.

They are built on the first, fourth and fifth notes of the scale. They are called the tonic, subdominant and dominant chords. The sad-sounding ones are the minor tonic triads.

The three-chord trick

You can harmonize a tune in any major scale by using the three major tonic triads. This is known as the three chord trick. These are the chords you use to harmonize a tune in C major:

G	C	D
E	A	B
C	F	G

Tonic (I)   Sub-dominant (IV)   Dominant (V)

Between them, these chords contain all the notes of the scale. To construct a simple harmony, you match the chords to the notes in the tune. Some notes occur in more than one of the chords. Here you can choose which chord sounds best.

The dominant triad often has the minor seventh note added to it, to give it extra spice. This chord is called the dominant seventh.

The dominant triad in the key of C major is G major. Here it has the minor seventh added.

You can harmonize many tunes in the following keys using the following sets of chords.

Dominant seventh chord symbol.

	I	IV	V⁷
G major	G	C	D⁷
F major	F	B♭	C⁷
D major	D	G	A⁷

Playing an accompaniment

Play this chord until a new one is indicated in the music.

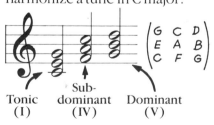

Swing low, sweet chariot
ⓒ   Ⓕ ⓒ
Coming for to carry me home
ⓒ   Ⓖ⁷
Swing low, sweet chariot
ⓒ   Ⓕ ⓒ
Coming for to carry me home
ⓒ   Ⓖ⁷   ⓒ

You don't have to play a different chord for every note in the tune. You can usually hear when you need to change the chord.

Musical instructions

Most composers write instructions in their music to tell you how to play it as they intended. Some of the most common signs and instructions are explained below.

Most of the written instructions are in Italian. This is because music was first printed in Italy and it became the custom for composers to use Italian instructions.

Signs in the music

Here are some symbols which tell you to play the notes in a certain way.

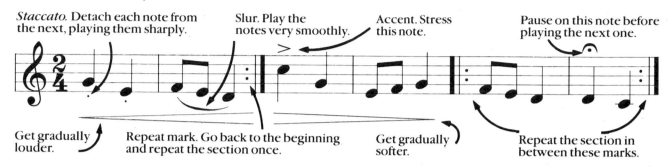

Staccato. Detach each note from the next, playing them sharply.

Slur. Play the notes very smoothly.

Accent. Stress this note.

Pause on this note before playing the next one.

Get gradually louder.

Repeat mark. Go back to the beginning and repeat the section once.

Get gradually softer.

Repeat the section in between these marks.

Tempo words

You may find these at the beginning of the music or where you need to change speed.

A tempo Return to the original speed.
Accelerando Speed up gradually.
Adagio Slow.
Affrettando Hurrying.
Allegretto Quite fast.
Allegro Lively and fast.
Andante At a walking pace.
Andantino At a fairly leisurely speed.
Grave Very slow.
Larghetto Almost as slow as largo.
Largo Slow and dignified.
Lento Slow.
Meno mosso Less movement.
Moderato Moderately paced.
Piu mosso More movement.
Prestissimo As fast as possible.
Presto Quick.
Rallentando (rall.) Gradually slowing down.
Ritardando (ritard.) Gradually slowing down.
Ritenuto Held back.
Tempo primo Return to the original tempo.
Vivace Quick and lively.

Mood and style

Agitato Agitatedly.
Animato With animation.
Appassionato With passion.
Brillante Sparkling.
Cantabile In a singing style.
Con bravura With boldness.
Con brio With vigour.
Con forza With power.
Con fuoco With fire.
Con moto With movement.
Dolce Sweetly.
Espressivo With expression.
Giocoso Merrily.
Grandioso Grandly.
Grazioso Gracefully.
Lacrimoso Sadly.
Legato Smoothly.
Legatissimo As smoothly as possible.
Leggiero Lightly.
Maestoso Majestically.
Marcato Marked, accented.
Perdendosi Dying away.
Pesante Heavily.
Risoluto Boldly.
Scherzando Playfully.
Sostenuto Very measured and smooth.
Spiritoso With animation.
Staccato Detach each note from the next.
Strepitoso Boisterously.
Vivace Lively and quickly.

Words describing volume

These instructions may be written as shown in brackets.

Crescendo (cresc) Getting gradually louder.
Decrescendo (decresc) Getting gradually softer.
Diminuendo (dim) Getting gradually softer.
Forte (f) Loud.
Fortissimo (ff) Very loud.
Mezzo forte (mf) Moderately loud.
Mezzo piano (mp) Moderately soft.
Pianissimo (pp) Very soft.
Piano (p) Soft.

More Italian words

Da capo (D.C.) Repeat from the beginning.
D.C. al Fine Repeat from the beginning, finishing at the word *Fine.*
Fine The end.
Glissando Slide between notes.
Meno Less.
Molto Much.
Piu More.
Poco a poco Little by little.
Sempre Always.
Senza Without.
Subito Suddenly.

FAMILIES OF INSTRUMENTS

All instruments are either acoustic or electrical. Sound is created on and amplified by the body of an acoustic instrument. Electrical instruments need a supply of electricity before they can make a musical sound.

Within these two groups, instruments belong to families depending on how they make sound. Acoustic instruments might belong to the strings, woodwind, brass, keyboard or percussion family. Electrical instruments are either electric or electronic.

These two pages list some of the instruments in these different families. Most of the instruments shown are orchestral and band instruments, with some popular music instruments and some from around the world included.

Woodwind instruments

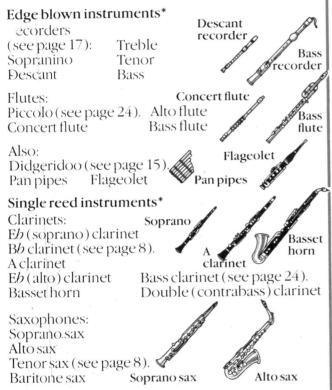

Edge blown instruments*

ecorders
(see page 17): Treble
Sopranino Tenor
Descant Bass

Descant recorder

Bass recorder

Flutes:
Piccolo (see page 24). Alto flute
Concert flute Bass flute

Concert flute

Bass flute

Also:
Didgeridoo (see page 15).
Pan pipes Flageolet

Flageolet

Pan pipes

Single reed instruments*

Clarinets:
E♭ (soprano) clarinet
B♭ clarinet (see page 8).
A clarinet
E♭ (alto) clarinet
Basset horn

Soprano

A clarinet

Basset horn

Bass clarinet (see page 24).
Double (contrabass) clarinet

Saxophones:
Soprano sax
Alto sax
Tenor sax (see page 8).
Baritone sax

Soprano sax

Alto sax

Double reed instruments*

Oboes:
Oboe
Cor anglais (see page 24).
Bassoon
Double or contrabassoon

Oboe

Bassoon

Free reed instruments

You do not put the reed directly in your mouth. Instead, you pump bellows or blow into a chamber where one or two reeds vibrate freely.

Bagpipes (see page 14).
Concertina (see page 14).
Accordion
Mouth organ

Accordion   Mouth organ

Brass instruments

The shape of the tube (bore) affects the tone of an instrument. The diameter of a cylindrical bore is about the same all the way down the tube, flaring into a bell shape at the end. A conical bore gets gradually wider.

Cylindrical bore instruments
A cylindrical bore produces a wave with lots of harmonics, giving a clear, bright tone.

Trumpets:
Natural (valveless) trumpet
Standard (B♭) trumpet
(see page 8).
Piccolo trumpet

Natural trumpet   Piccolo trumpet

Trombones:
Tenor trombone (see page 8).
Tenor/bass trombone

Tenor/bass trombone

Conical bore instruments
A conical bore reduces the number of harmonics, producing a fuller and less bright tone.

French or double horn
Bugle
B♭ cornet
B♭ flügelhorn

French horn   Bugle   Cornet

Saxhorns:
E♭ tenor horn
B♭ baritone
B♭ tenor tuba
or euphonium
E♭ bass tuba

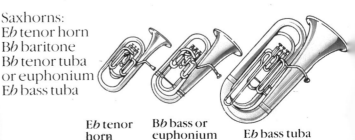

E♭ tenor horn   B♭ bass or euphonium   E♭ bass tuba

Stringed instruments

You produce sound from a stringed instrument by making a string vibrate (see page 30).

Violins:
Violin (see page 30).
Viola (see page 23).
Cello (see page 23).
Double bass (see page 30).

Viols (see page 17):
Viola d'amore
Viola da gamba

Harps and zithers:
Koto
Zither (see page 30).
Harp (see page 30).

Guitars and lutes:
Acoustic guitar (see page 31).
Lute (see page 17).
Balalaika (see page 14).
Mandolin (see page 30).
Banjo (see page 14).
Sitar (see page 14).
Vina (see page 14.)
Tambura (see page 33).
Ukelele

Viola   Cello   Viola da gamba   Koto   Harp   Balalaika   Banjo   Ukelele

Keyboard instruments

Keyboard instruments divide up into those which make sounds from vibrating strings and those which make sound from a vibrating column of air.

Stringed keyboard instruments:
Clavichord
Harpsichord (see page 20).
Upright piano
Grand piano (see page 24).

Clavichord

Wind keyboard instruments:
Pipe organ (see page 21).
Harmonium

Harmonium

Percussion

Percussion instruments are either tuned (producing a musical note) or untuned (producing noise). See page 30.

Untuned percussion
Drums:
Side or snare drum
Tom-tom (see page 30).
Tenor drum
Bass drum (see page 30).
Bongos   Conga   Timbales

Bongos   Conga   Timbales

Clappers:
Claves (see page 30).
Castanets   Whip (slapstick)

Castanets   Slapstick

Rattles: Slit drums:
Maracas   Wood block
Cabaca   Log drum

Cabaca   Wood block

Cymbals:
Clash cymbals
Crash cymbals (see page 30).
Hi-hat cymbals (see page 30).

Finger cymbals   Clash cymbals   Finger cymbals

Also:
Gong or tamtam
Tambourine
Triangle
Wind machine
Guiro

Gong   Wind machine   Guiro

Tuned percussion
Xylophones:
Xylophone
Marimba

Xylophone   Marimba

Metallophones:
Vibraphone
Glockenspiel
Celesta

Vibraphone   Glockenspiel

Chimes:
Tubular bells
Chime bars   Cowbells

Chime bars   Tubular bells

Also:
Timpani
Steel drums (see page 30).

Timpani

Electric instruments
On an electric instrument, the sound is amplified electronically rather than by the body of the instrument.

Electric guitar (see page 31).
Bass guitar (see page 8).
Electric organ
Electric violin

Electric violin

Electronic instruments
An electronic instrument creates a sound purely electronically, without any acoustic means (see page 29).

Keyboard synthesizer (see page 29).
Drum synthesizer (see page 29)
Ondes Martenot

Ondes Martenot

LEARNING AN INSTRUMENT

Many music lessons are geared towards teaching a student how to play and read written music, mainly classical. This does not help the student learn how to improvise or create music. This may not matter to a classical player but jazz musicians, for instance, need to be able to improvise. Some classical teachers, though, are sympathetic to other styles and can help you develop your skills in them.

Finding a teacher

Your local library probably has a list of music teachers in your area. A music shop may also know of local teachers, or carry their advertisements.

For recommendations, you could ask the music staff at your school or college. If possible, talk to a teacher's existing pupils to get an idea of what he or she is like and what kind of training is provided.

Some teachers, especially those of the less common instruments, may be professional orchestral musicians who teach in their spare time.

Acquiring an instrument

You may be able to borrow a school instrument, especially if the school band or orchestra needs players of that instrument. Brass bands usually lend instruments to junior members on long-term loan.

Instruments are expensive to buy. There is a rough guide to the relative costs of new beginner's quality instruments in the chart on the opposite page. Whether you buy new or second hand, get some insurance in case you lose or damage the instrument.

Buying new

To help with the cost of buying a new instrument, most music shops operate a lease purchase scheme. This involves paying a certain sum per month as rental. After a few months, if you decide to buy the instrument, most of the rental is deducted from the price.

Generally, the more you pay, the better the instrument. Most instruments hold their value well for future sale second-hand. Electric instruments, though, depreciate quickly.

Buying second hand

It is vital to have a second-hand instrument checked by someone who knows about it before you buy it. A teacher or reputable music shop will probably do this for a fee.

Some music shops sell second-hand instruments. They should let you have one on approval. Be suspicious if they are unwilling to provide a year's guarantee. You may see advertisements for instruments in the local press but these do not have a guarantee.

Check List
(For new and second hand instruments).
1 Get a guarantee
2 Have the instrument checked
3 Insure it

Choosing an instrument

If you are interested in learning an instrument, the points below and the chart on the opposite page might help you to pick a suitable one.

★Ask yourself whether you would prefer to play in a band or orchestra, or play a self-contained instrument such as a classical guitar or piano. Some instruments such as flutes and violins can be played both on their own and in groups.

★If you choose a group instrument, make sure there is a local group that you can join when you are good enough. Contact the group to see what instruments they are short of.

★You may be able to join a group class for some instruments. These are cheaper than individual lessons. Brass instruments are fairly cheap to learn because most coaching is carried out at band practices.

★In general, the more complex an instrument looks, the easier it is to play the right note. For instance, it is easier to pitch notes on a saxophone than a violin because there are more mechanical aids to help you.

★It is easier to read the music for an instrument that can only play one note at a time than for an instrument that can play several notes at once, such as a piano or harp.

Choosing an instrument: chart

COST*	POTENTIAL	EASE OF PLAYING
Flute Moderate	The flute has lots of classical solo, orchestral and piano duet music as well as folk music.	The flute is quite easy for beginners unless you are left-handed. Very thick or very thin lips, or large front teeth, can make it difficult to blow.
Clarinet Moderate	Clarinets are needed in orchestras and bands and may have solo parts within these.	It is easier to blow than the flute and you can make progress quite quickly. Strong front teeth which would hamper flute-playing are a positive advantage.
Oboe Very expensive	The oboe is an orchestral instrument with some solo parts.	The oboe is difficult. It helps to have thin lips which you can fold over your teeth to grip the reed.
Saxophone Expensive	Saxes are needed in jazz and dance bands. There is some 20th century classical music for saxophones.	A sax is easier than a flute or clarinet. It is a good choice if you are not very interested in classical music.
Recorder Very cheap	On your own, you can play any single-line music. There is also lots of music for recorder groups.	Basic technique is not too difficult although early attempts can be discouraging. Advanced technique needs a lot of skill.
Cornet Expensive	This is the lead instrument in a brass band. Some orchestras have cornets as well as trumpets.	A cornet is quite light and easy to blow. It is a good brass instrument to start on.
Trumpet Moderate	Trumpets often lead in dance and jazz bands. They are also orchestral instruments.	A trumpet is harder to blow than a cornet, but it makes a stronger and brighter sound. You need to be bold as you cannot hide your mistakes.
Tenor horn and baritone Expensive	These are brass band instruments for people who like group music.	These demand the least energy of all the brass. The music is mostly not difficult.
Trombone Moderate	This is needed by orchestras, dance bands, brass bands, jazz groups and brass chamber groups.	You need a good sense of pitch to find each note. You don't need good finger control, though. You may need fleshier lips than a cornet or trumpet player.
Euphonium Expensive	This is second in importance to the cornet in a brass band.	The euphonium requires a lot of puff and it helps to be quite large.
Tuba (E♭ or B♭ bass) Very expensive	This is an orchestral and a brass band instrument. It usually provides the bass foundation.	The tuba is big but needs less puff than a trumpet. The music is not difficult and you rarely have to play fast.
French horn Very expensive.	This orchestral and solo instrument has a greater role in classical music than any other brass.	It is the hardest brass instrument to play and is not usually recommended as a first instrument. It helps to have thin to medium lips.
Violin Moderate	There is lots of orchestral and solo classical violin music. For a change you can play folk fiddle.	It is not easy to make nice sounds on a violin. It may be a year or two before you can produce a really good tone.
Viola Moderate	There are lots of orchestral and chamber music parts for viola plus some 20th century solo works.	Most viola music is easier than violin music but your fingers have to move further on the larger instrument. Long arms and fingers are an advantage.
Cello Expensive	There is masses of chamber, orchestral and solo cello music.	The cello is easier for beginners than the violin but the advanced technique requires the same skill.
Double bass Very expensive	This is an orchestral instrument which is also found in the rhythm section of dance and jazz bands.	Most (but not all) of the orchestral music is quite simple. The double bass can play solos in jazz bands. It helps to have strong, quite large hands.
Classical guitar Cheap	The classical guitar is not a group instrument but the solo repertoire is huge.	Classical guitar is not easy to play. Your fingers need to do different things quickly and with great precision.
Electric and bass guitar Moderate	Electric guitars are mostly needed in rock bands. Basses may also be found in dance and big bands.	It is not difficult to pick up chord technique, strumming and picking on an electric guitar. A bass is quite easy as you play only one note at a time.
Drums A kit is expensive.	A drummer/percussionist can play in orchestras, rock and jazz groups, dance and brass bands.	Learning to play drums well takes several years. You need a perfect sense of rhythm. You can use a practice pad to muffle the sound of a drum.
Piano Extremely expensive	There is masses of all sorts of piano music. The technique gives you a start on other keyboards.	It is not easy to read and play several notes at once. Still, to sound a note you just have to press it, so anyone can pick out tunes and harmonies.

In this chart, a moderately priced instrument might cost you about as much as a new bicycle. An expensive instrument might cost up to twice as much and a very expensive one twice as much again.

COMPOSERS IN CONTEXT

The chart on the next four pages tells you a little about a number of composers, the kind of music they wrote and when they were composing. The list can only cover a selection of composers, so don't expect to find every composer in it. It also tells you if a composer or their music is mentioned elsewhere in the book.

Machaut, Guillaume de
c.1300-1377
France
(See page 17.)

His works show how music was developing in the 14th century, with greater variety of rhythm and melody and more independent movement of parts than before.

Dunstable, John
c.1380/90-1453
England

He wrote mostly church music. His ornamental style influenced French composers of this period.

Josquin des Prez
c.1440-1521
Netherlands
(See page 17.)

A distinguished church musician, he composed both sacred and secular music.

Tallis, Thomas
c.1505-1585
England
(See pages 17 and 37.)

Several of Tallis' tunes still exist as hymn tunes. He wrote instrumental pieces and madrigals as well as church music.

Palestrina, Giovanni da
c.1525-1594
Italy
(See page 17.)

He took his name from his native town, Palestrina. He is famous for his unaccompanied vocal polyphonic music.

Lassus, Roland de
c.1532-1594
Belgium

Lassus was a favorite in various European courts. His large output included many splendid motets.

Byrd, William
c.1543-1623
England
(See page 37.)

A famous Elizabethan organist and composer, Byrd wrote church music, songs and music for keyboard and viol consorts.

Morley, Thomas
1557-1603
England
(See page 37.)

A pupil of William Byrd, Morley's output included church music, instrumental music for consorts, keyboard pieces and madrigals.

Sweelinck, Jan Pieterzoon
1562-1621
Netherlands

He is mainly remembered for his organ and harpsichord pieces, from which Bach learned a lot.

Dowland, John
1563-1626
England

He was a great lute music composer and wrote over 800 lute-songs. He also wrote for consorts of viols.

Monteverdi, Claudio
1567-1643
Italy
(See pages 37, 38 and 40.)

Monteverdi was the first great opera composer. He wrote in a new harmonic style which enabled the words to be grasped more easily than earlier polyphonic styles.

Gibbons, Orlando
1583-1625
England
(See page 37.)

Gibbons was a skilled keyboard player. He wrote for viols and virginals (an early keyboard) and composed madrigals, motets and anthems.

Schütz, Heinrich
1585-1672
Germany

Schütz was one of the greatest composers of church music before the time of Bach.

Lully, Jean-Baptiste
1632-1687
France
(See page 39.)

Lully was born in Italy and became a violinist, composer, actor, dancer and conductor. He worked in the court of Louis XIV, writing operas, ballets and church music.

Buxtehude, Dietrich
1637-1707
Denmark

Bach heard Buxtehude play the organ and learned much from his style. Buxtehude also wrote cantatas for the church.

Corelli, Arcangelo
1653-1713
Italy
(See page 21.)

Corelli wrote skilfully for the violin, which was replacing the viol as the main stringed instrument. He developed the *concerto grosso* form, influencing other composers.

Purcell, Henry
1659-1695
England
(See page 21.)

Purcell wrote church and ceremonial music, songs, consort and keyboard pieces and an opera, *Dido and Aeneas*.

Couperin, François
1668-1733
France

Couperin performed brilliantly on organ and harpsichord and wrote attractive pieces for them, such as his set of harpsichord suites.

Vivaldi, Antonio
c.1676-1741
Italy

Vivaldi wrote nearly 400 *concerti grossi*. He also composed nearly 40 operas besides his church music.

Telemann, Georg Philipp
1681-1767
Germany

Telemann's large and varied musical output was considered more modern and rated more highly than Bach's at the time.

Bach, Johann Sebastian
1685-1750
Germany
(See pages 20, 21 and 37.)

The master of baroque polyphony, Bach wrote for clavichord, organ, violin and cello. He wrote suites and concertos for the orchestra. Choral works include the *B Minor Mass* and *St Matthew Passion*.

Handel, George Frideric
1685-1759
Germany
(See pages 20 and 21.)

He was a great harpsichord player and organist. The clear outlines of his music were admired by later composers such as Beethoven and Mozart. He composed a lot of music including opera and oratorio.

Scarlatti, Domenico
1685-1757
Italy

Scarlatti's best-known works are the harpsichord sonatas, of which he wrote 555.

Haydn, Franz Josef
1732-1809
Austria
(See page 23.)

He developed the symphony and sonata and made Classical chamber music fashionable. He wrote 104 symphonies. He befriended Mozart and taught Beethoven.

Mozart, Wolfgang Amadeus
1756-1791
Austria (See page 23, 37, 40.)

Mozart wrote over 600 works before he died aged 35. As a child he was a brilliant pianist. By his late teens he was writing mature and elegant symphonies, concertos, operas, Masses and chamber music.

von Paradis, Maria Theresia 1759-1824 Austria — She composed operas, chamber music, keyboard pieces and songs but her best-known work is the *Sicilienne* for violin and piano.

Beethove, Ludwig van 1770-1827 Germany (See page 23.) — He was a lonely genius whose career as a virtuoso pianist was cut short by early deafness. His powerful style of composing, particularly in the symphonies and piano sonatas, caused a stir in late Classical times.

Weber, Carl Maria von 1786-1826 Germany — He is best remembered for the colourful overtures to his operas, especially to *Der Freischütz* and *Oberon*.

Rossini, Gioacchino 1792-1868 Italy (See page 40.) — His operas, such as *The Barber of Seville*, earned him a fortune. *The Wlliam Tell Overture* is probably his best known work. He also wrote instrumental and chamber music,

Donizetti, Gaetano 1797-1848 Italy — His popularity rests on his operas, of which he wrote about 70. *Don Pasquale* is probably the best known.

Schubert, Franz Peter 1797-1828 Austria (See page 37.) — He was a great songwriter but was just becoming famous when he died aged 31. His string quartets and later symphonies (the *Unfinished Symphony* and the *Ninth ("Great") Symphony in C Major*) are popular.

Berlioz, (Louis) Hector 1803-1869 France (See page 24.) — He was a brilliant and eccentric composer of highly Romantic music. Some of his choral and orchestral music required hundreds of performers.

Mendelssohn, Felix 1809-1847 Germany — He was a pianist, organist and conductor who began composing in his early teens. He wrote eight books of *Songs Without Words* for piano which earned him popularity.

Schumann, Robert 1810-1856 Germany (See pages 25 and 37.) — He was a true Romantic, using music to reflect and inspire emotions. He composed songs and piano pieces, four symphonies, chamber works and concertos.

Chopin, Frederic 1810-1849 Poland (See page 25.) — Chopin was proud to be Polish (his father was born French but was Polish by adoption). He wrote many piano pieces such as nocturnes, mazurkas and polonaises.

Liszt, Franz 1811-1886 Hungary (See page 25.) — By the age of 9, Liszt was a piano virtuoso. His fame rests mostly on his showy and difficult piano works. He is largely responsible for inventing the symphonic poem.

Wagner, (Wilhelm) Richard 1813-1883 Germany (See pages 39, 40.) — His operas, which he called music-dramas, are still performed all over the world. His original use of harmony, orchestration and the human voice had a startling effect on the world of music.

Verdi, Giuseppe 1813-1901 Italy (See pages 39, 40.) — Verdi's music made him a national hero. Apart from his great *Requiem Mass*, his reputation rests almost entirely on his operas.

Offenbach, Jacques 1819-1880 France (See pages 39 and 40.) — He was a cellist, conductor and theatre manager. He wrote very popular operettas (see page 39) and ballet music.

Franck, César 1822-1890 Belgium (See page 43.) — He was an organist who worked in Paris. He wrote organ, piano, instrumental and orchestral works, an opera, oratorios and church music.

Bruckner, Anton 1824-1896 Austria — He was a cathedral and court organist and recitalist. His most impressive works are his large-scale symphonies.

Smetana, Bedřich 1824-1884 Bohemia (now Czechoslovakia) (See page 25.) — Mainly self-taught, he became a music teacher and conductor in Prague and is regarded by Czechs as their first national composer. He wrote songs and orchestral music. His best-known opera is *The Bartered Bride*.

Strauss II, Johann 1825-1899 Austria (See page 40.) — He is known as The Waltz King of Vienna due to his light music. His father Johann I, brothers Joseph and Eduard and nephew Johann III were also successful in this field.

Borodin, Alexander 1833-1887 Russia (See page 25.) — He was a chemist and lack of time meant that some of his music had to be completed by others. Rimsky-Korsakov and Glazounov edited his spectacular opera *Prince Igor*.

Brahms, Johannes 1833-1897 Germany (See page 25.) — His music is Romantic but in a Classical mold. He wrote piano solos, chamber music, songs, choral music, concertos and four symphonies. He had high standards and destroyed much of his music.

Delibes, Léo 1836-1891 France — He is remembered for his music to the ballet *Coppélia* and for a piece called *Pizzicato* from the ballet *Sylvia*.

Bizet, Georges 1838-1875 France (See page 39.) — His well-written and tuneful music did not become popular until after his early death. Even his opera *Carmen* was a flop to begin with.

Mussorgsky, Modeste 1839-1881 Russia (See page 24.) — He left the army for a career as a pianist and composer. His songs, choral works, operas (such as *Boris Godunof*) and orchestral pieces are unmistakably Russian.

Tchaikovsky, Peter Ilich (1840-1893) Russia (See page 24.) — His rich orchestral writing won him great popularity. He is well-known for his ballet music.

Dvořák, Antonín 1841-1904 Bohemia (now Czechoslovakia) (See page 25.) — He played the viola and organ and wrote tuneful works of all kinds. The *Largo* from his *New World Symphony* and the *Humoresque No. 7* are among the best known.

Sullivan, (Sir) Arthur
1842-1900
England

His serious chamber, orchestral and religious music is seldom heard but his light operas, written with W.S. Gilbert (the librettist), are popular.

Grieg, Edvard
1843-1907
Norway
(See page 25.)

The demand for quite easy drawing-room piano pieces grew in the 19th century. Grieg wrote many of these as well as songs, a piano concerto and music for Ibsen's play *Peer Gynt*.

Rimsky-Korsakov, Nicholas
1844-1908
Russia (See pages 24, 25.)

Rimsky-Korsakov was interested in folk song and was an important Nationalist composer. His orchestral pieces, such as *Capriccio Espagnole* and *Scheherezade*, are lavish and colourful.

Fauré, Gabriel
1845-1924
France

Fauré was a church organist and choirmaster. He was best at writing songs and chamber music. His *Requiem Mass* is very beautiful.

Janáček, Leoš
1854-1928
Moravia (now Czechoslovakia)
(See pages 26, 27 and 37.)

He was fascinated by the sounds of nature, folksong and speech. He wrote operas and instrumental, chamber and orchestral works, all highly individual.

Elgar, Edward William
1857-1934
England
(See page 25.)

Elgar was the greatest English composer since Purcell. The *Enigma Variations* followed by the oratorio *The Dream of Gerontius* established his reputation.

Puccini, Giacomo
1858-1924
Italy

Puccini is best-known as a successful composer of Italian grand opera (see pages 39 and 40).

Mahler, Gustav
1860-1911
Bohemia (now Czechoslovakia)
(See pages 26 and 27.)

Mahler was a pupil of Bruckner and a great conductor of opera. He wrote nine symphonies and his song cycles are also highly regarded.

Debussy, Claude
1862-1918
France
(See pages 26 and 27.)

Debussy disregarded the rules of harmony, often using modes and whole-tone scales. This gave some of his music an oriental flavour. His orchestral prelude *L'Après-midi d'un Faune* is well known.

Strauss, Richard
1864-1949
Germany
(See pages 27 and 37.)

Strauss enjoyed writing for large symphony orchestras. Of his operas, *Der Rosenkavalier* is the best known. He is also famous for his symphonic poems and *Lieder*.

Sibelius, Jean
1865-1957
Finland
(See page 25.)

Aged 32, he received a pension so he could devote himself to composing. His great works are his symphonies, his violin concerto and the tone poems inspired by Finnish sagas.

Satie, Erik
1866-1925
France

A café pianist and friend of Debussy, Satie could write both light and serious works. He led young French composers away from the heavy Wagnerian Romantic style.

Joplin, Scott
1868-1917
USA
(See page 43.)

Joplin's name is linked with ragtime (see page 10). Two of his best-known piano rags are the *Maple Leaf Rag* and *The Entertainer*.

Vaughan Williams, Ralph
1872-1958
England
(See page 27.)

Vaughan Williams' love for early English music and folk song is evident in pieces such as the *Fantasia on a Theme of Thomas Tallis* and the *Fantasia on Greensleeves*.

Rachmaninov, Sergei
1873-1943
Russia

He wrote four piano concertos, later used as film music. Famous works are the *Prelude in C Sharp Minor* for piano (written when he was 19) and *Rhapsody on a Theme of Paganini* for piano and orchestra.

Holst, Gustav
1874-1934
England
(See page 26.)

His interest in folk music, astrology and eastern religions is reflected in his music. His suite *The Planets* is an example of his brilliant orchestration.

Ives, Charles
1874-1954
USA

His music often incorporated popular tunes and hymns. He was ahead of his time with experiments in polytonality and serialism. Some see him as the first truly "American" composer.

Schoenberg, Arnold
1874-1951
Germany (See pages 26, 27.)

Schoenberg was a major figure in 20th century music. His numerous pupils adopted his revolutionary techniques, using a 12-note scale instead of the usual key system.

Ravel, Maurice
1875-1937
France
(See pages 26 and 27.)

Ravel's style was Romantic and showed his interest in Spanish music. It was occasionally influenced by jazz. *Bolero* shows his colourful, spectacular use of the orchestra.

Falla, Manuel de
1876-1946
Spain
(See pages 25 and 43.)

Falla was a great composer of real Spanish music. *The Ritual Fire Dance* is a popular example. He also wrote for Diaghilev's ballet company, the *Ballet Russe*.

Bartók, Béla
1881-1945
Hungary
(See page 25.)

Bartók's study of the folk music of Hungary, Rumania and Bulgaria is evident in many of his works. His large output of piano music is graded and much of it is very difficult.

Grainger, Percy
1882-1961
Australia

His style was high-spirited and he incorporated folk music in his work, especially in songs and piano pieces.

Kodály, Zoltán
1882-1967
Hungary
(See page 25.)

With Bartók, he collected masses of folk music and his music reflects this. Among his best-known works are the orchestral suite *Háry János* and the *Psalmus Hungaricus*.

Stravinsky, Igor
1882-1971
Russia
(See pages 27 and 43.)

He wrote music in many styles. His symphonies are large in scale and very expressive. He wrote music for Diaghilev's *Ballet Russe*, now in the repertoire of many companies.

Bax, Arnold
1883-1953
England

His work includes songs, piano and chamber music and symphonies. It has a romantic, Celtic flavour (for instance, in the tone poem *Tintagel*).

Berg, Alban
1885-1935
Austria
(See page 26.)

Like his teacher Schoenberg, he used the 12-note system but rather more flexibly. Two great works are his violin concerto and the opera *Wozzeck*.

Kern, Jerome
1885-1945
USA

He is regarded as the first composer of the musical. His best-known musical is probably *Showboat* (1928).

Berlin, Irving
1888-1989
USA

He was born in Russia but spent most of his life in the USA. His tunes, such as *God Bless America*, were singable and popular. He wrote musicals such as *Annie Get Your Gun* (1950).

Porter, Cole
1891-1964
USA

Porter began composing aged eight. He wrote witty words for his many songs. Of his musicals, *Kiss Me Kate* was particularly successful.

Prokofiev, Serge
1891-1953
Russia
(See pages 27 and 43.)

He studied composition under Rimsky-Korsakov. He was interested in pre-Romantic musical forms. He wrote eight fine piano sonatas. He was one of the most prolific ballet composers of 20th century.

Hindemith, Paul
1895-1963
Germany

Though influenced by serialism, Hindemith felt music should be acceptable to the average person and that composers should not neglect writing for children and amateurs. (See *Everyday Music*, page 27.)

Gershwin, George
1898-1937
USA
(See page 40.)

He was a jazz pianist before studying composition. He used jazz elements in his symphonic music. Famous works are *Rhapsody in Blue* and the opera *Porgy and Bess*.

Coward, (Sir) Noel
1899-1973
England

He was a composer, playwright and actor. He could play and compose at the piano by ear. He wrote both music and witty lyrics for songs such as *Mad Dogs and Englishmen*.

Copland, Aaron
Born 1900
USA
(See page 43.)

His wide musical interests, ranging from Stravinsky to jazz and folk, are evident in his own music. His ballet music and the orchestral piece *El Salon Mexico* are often played.

Rodgers, Richard
1902-1980
USA
(See page 40.)

He was a songwriter and composer of light music. His later musicals, written with Oscar Hammerstein, included *Oklahoma!* (1943), *South Pacific* (1949) and *The Sound of Music* (1965).

Walton, (Sir) William
1902-1983
England

Walton composed opera and choral works but was particularly successful with orchestral works. He is well-known for the witty *Façade Suite*.

Tippett, (Sir) Michael
Born 1905
England
(See page 37.)

His work seems to have roots in the 17th century and earlier but he also uses jazz elements. He composed for piano, organ, chamber groups and orchestra as well as vocal works.

Lutyens (Agnes) Elizabeth
1906-1983
England

She composed a variety of music including works for cinema and radio. She wrote some of her own texts for her vocal music.

Shostakovich, Dmitri
1906-1975
Russia

He began composing aged nine, before the Russian Revolution, but became a leading composer in the USSR. Of his 15 symphonies, the *Tenth* is probably the finest.

Messiaen, Olivier
Born 1908
France

Messiaen's Catholic faith and his interest in bird song and oriental music are all vital forces in his work. The *Turangalila Symphony* is one of his greatest achievements.

Cage, John
Born 1912
USA
(See page 27.)

A pupil of Schoenberg, Cage composes experimental music. He has used such items as radios to provide unpredictability in his music.

Britten, (Lord) Benjamin
1913-1976
England
(See pages 37 and 39.)

Britten admired Stravinsky but avoided the atonality of the Schoenberg school. He drew inspiration from the sea and wrote several pieces for children to perform, such as *Noye's Fludde*.

Bernstein, Leonard
Born 1918
USA

Influenced by Shostakovich and Mahler, he draws from jazz and Jewish sacred music. He is famous for his musical *West Side Story* (1957).

Berio, Luciano
Born 1925
Italy
(See page 37.)

He has produced fascinating effects using the voice and electronic instruments. Some of his works, such as *Circles*, require the performers to move about and so are best seen live.

Stockhausen, Karlheinz
Born 1928
Germany
(See page 27.)

Stockhausen is famous for his creative use of electronic instruments which he sometimes combines with the voice to produce unexpected effects.

Williamson, Malcolm
Born 1931
Australia

He has used serialism (see page 26). His output includes a symphony, piano pieces, church music and operas. In some works the audience is required to take part.

Birtwistle, (Sir) Harrison
Born 1934
England

Birtwistle has written operas, vocal, instrumental and orchestral pieces. Some of his music contains aleatoric (chance) effects.

Maxwell Davies, (Sir) Peter
Born 1934
England

He and Birtwistle were fellow students. His earlier works were very modern but latterly his interest in 16th century music is reflected.

Lennon, John
1940-1980
England
(See page 5.)

Some of his songs, such as *Help*, were written with Paul McCartney. Others, such as *Imagine* which appeared in 1971 after the Beatles had been disbanded, were his own.

Le Fanu, Nicola
Born 1947
England

The daughter of composer Elizabeth Maconchy, she has written a variety of instrumental, orchestral and vocal works as well as theatre music.

Lloyd Webber, Andrew
Born 1948
England
(See page 39.)

Lloyd Webber has composed music for a long list of very successful musicals including *Jesus Christ Superstar*, *Evita*, *Cats*, *The Phantom of the Opera* and *Aspects of Love*.

GLOSSARY

If you cannot find the word you are looking for in the glossary below, look it up in the index. It may be described elsewhere in the book. Words in italics are explained elsewhere in the glossary.

Acoustic instruments Instruments designed to produce and amplify sounds without the help of electricity.

Acoustics The study of how sound behaves.

Aleatoric music Music which has an element of chance in it.

Alto The *vocal range* of the lowest female or boy's voice.

Anthem A choral work for singing in church.

Aria A vocal solo within an opera or *oratorio*.

Atonal Describes music with no relationship to a key.

Baritone The male *vocal range* between the *tenor* and *bass*.

Baroque music Intricate styles of music, written between about 1600 and 1750.

Bass The lowest male *vocal range*.

Basso continuo Symbols written above or beneath the *stave* which indicate a series of chords from which a harpsichordist can improvise an accompaniment. This was a 17th and 18th century practice.

Bitonal Describes music written in two keys.

Cadenza A showy passage within a concerto during which a soloist plays alone.

Canon A piece where more than one voice or instrument play the same theme but at different times, making patterns.

Cantata A piece of vocal music for a soloist or choir.

Chamber music Music for a small group of instruments, each playing a separate part.

Chorale A type of early Protestant hymn.

Chromatic scale A *scale* of 12 notes, each a semitone apart.

Chromaticism The inclusion of notes not part of the key in which a piece of music is written.

Classical music A general term describing formal or religious music. More specifically, it is formal music from about 1750 to 1820 in which musical form was more important than emotional expression.

Concert pitch A standard pitch based on a frequency of 440 cps for the A above Middle C.

Concerto A *sonata* for a solo instrument, or instruments, accompanied by an orchestra.

Concerto grosso An early form of *concerto* in which a small group of instruments is contrasted with a larger group.

Continuo An instrument or group that accompanies a soloist, especially in *baroque music*.

Contralto See *alto*.

Counter tenor The falsetto male *vocal range*: the same as the female *alto*.

Diatonic Describes a set of notes that belong to a major or minor *scale*.

Dynamics The contrast between loud and soft within a piece of music.

Figured bass See *basso continuo*.

Front line The instruments in a jazz band which play the tune and take turns to *improvise*.

Gebrauchsmusik (German for utility music.) An early 20th century style intended to appeal to the majority, not just the musically sophisticated.

Harmonic Subsidiary waves produced, for instance, by a string vibrating not just along its whole length (producing the main note) but along fractions of its length. These harmonics give an instrument its *timbre*.

Head arrangement An outline of a piece of jazz music, showing which instruments should play and for how many bars.

Impressionism A movement in art and music during the late 19th and early 20th century. Impressionist works conveyed atmosphere and feeling rather than accurate detail.

Improvisation Spontaneous invention and performance.

Instrumentation The choice of instruments for a piece of music.

Jam session An opportunity for jazz musicians to work out the structure of a piece and *improvise* together.

Leitmotif (German for leading motive.) A theme representing a person, object or idea.

Libretto The words of an opera or *oratorio*.

Lieder (German for songs.) The name is applied mainly to 19th century songs for soloist with piano accompaniment.

Madrigal An unaccompanied part song for two to six voices, popular during the Renaissance.

Mezzo-soprano The middle female *vocal range*, between the *soprano* and the *alto* range.

MIDI See *Musical Instrument Digital Interface*.

Minimal music A style developed in the 1950s, consisting of a repeated phrase which gradually changes.

Modes *Scales* used by the Ancient Greeks which use only the white notes on a keyboard. *Plainsong*, Eastern music and some folk music uses modes.

Modulation The changing of key during a piece of music.

Monophony Music made up of a single line with no harmonies.

Multitracking A method of sound recording in which different instruments or parts are recorded on to separate tracks on the tape. They are mixed together later to achieve the desired balance of sound.

Music drama A type of opera developed by Wagner in which music, words, acting and scenery all combine to form a dramatic whole. The music is continuous.

Musical Instrument Digital Interface Electronic circuitry which interprets signals from one piece of electronic music equipment for another, so that more than one piece can be controlled from one place.

Musique concrète A style developed in the 1950s which involved taping natural sounds and then manipulating and combining them on tape.

Mute A device fitted to an instrument which muffles or changes its tone by reducing *harmonics* and *resonance*.

Nationalism A late 19th century movement. Composers wrote music based on or including elements from folk music, to give it a national flavour.

Neo-classical music A style of 20th century music in which composers expressed modern *tonality* and harmony but used *Classical* forms.

Note row The 12 notes in a *chromatic scale* arranged and used as the basis for a piece of *serial music*.

Opus Latin word for work. Opus numbers on musical works show the order of composition or publication.

Oratorio A musical work for soloists, choir and orchestra usually on a religious theme.

Orchestration The arrangement of a piece of music for an orchestra.

Pentatonic scale A five-note *scale*.

Plainsong Early *monophonic* church music consisting of sung Latin services.

Polyphony Music consisting of a number of different tunes which move independently but which weave together to form a harmonious whole.

Polyrhythm A number of different rhythms which fit together to form patterns.

Polytonality The use of several different keys at once.

Process music See *Minimal music*.

Programme music *Romantic music* which tells a story or describes a scene.

Ragas Sets of notes used as bases for improvisation in Indian music.

Recitative A style of solo singing which uses the rhythms and inflexions of speech. Recitative is used in opera and *oratorio* for dialogue or narrative.

Resolution The following of one chord by another which brings a phrase to a satisfactory close.

Resonance The vibration of an object in response to sound wave vibrations close to it. This amplifies the sound wave.

Rhythm section Instruments in a jazz band which provide the rhythm and *improvise* around it.

Romantic music Music inspired by the Romantic movement in the 19th century. Emotional content or supernatural themes were considered more desirable than musical form.

Round A simple sung *canon*.

Scale A set of notes on which a piece of music can be based. The scale is identified by the pattern of *intervals* between the notes.

Serial music Music consisting of a *note row* repeated in various ways.

Sonata Three or four pieces, or movements, put together. Most sonatas are for small groups of instruments.

Song cycle A set of songs linked by a theme or telling a story.

Soprano The highest female *vocal range*, equivalent to the boy's treble.

Soundbox The body of an instrument designed to amplify the sound the instrument produces.

Sprechgesang (German for speech song.) A style of singing which combines speech rhythms and tones with singing techniques.

Sprechstimme (German for speaking voice.) See *sprechgesang*.

Staff A set of five lines on which music can be written.

Suite A set of separate pieces designed to be played in sequence.

Sympathetic strings Strings which *resonate* when other strings on the same instrument are plucked or bowed.

Symphonic poem A long work of *programme music* not divided into movements.

Symphony A set of movements usually linked by a theme for an orchestra.

Syncopation The placing of an emphasis in an unusual place in the bar, such as just before or after a beat. This gives music interesting tensions and life.

Talas Rhythm patterns used in Indian music.

Tenor The highest broken male *vocal range*.

Thorough bass See *basso continuo*.

Timbre The characteristic tone quality of an instrument.

Tonality The relationship of a piece of music to a *scale*.

Tone poem See *symphonic poem*.

Tone row See *Note row*.

Treble The *vocal range* of an unbroken boy's voice.

Variation The development of a theme by adapting it.

Vibrato A rapid, small variation in the pitch of note.

Virtuoso A brilliant instrumentalist.

Vocal range The difference in pitch between the lowest note a person can sing and the highest.

Whole-tone scale A *scale* consisting of six notes, with a tone between each one.

INDEX

Acknowledgements

Music setting by Poco Ltd.

Cover photographs, top row: Redferns/David Redfern; third row: Redferns/Tim Hall; second and bottom row: Clive Barda; page 4: Redferns/Rudi Reiner; page 5, top: Redferns/William Gottlieb; bottom: Redferns/David Redfern; page 6: Redferns/David Redfern; page 10: Redferns/William Gottlieb; page 11, top and centre left: Redferns/William Gottlieb; others: Redferns/David Redfern; page 12, top: Redferns/David Redfern; centre: Redferns/Tim Hall; bottom: Redferns/William Gottlieb; page 15: Redferns/David Redfern; page 35, left: Redferns/David Redfern; centre: Redferns/William Gottlieb; right: Redferns/Rudi Reiner; page 38, top: Clive Barda; bottom: courtesy of the Royal Opera House; page 39, centre bottom: Catherine Ashmore; others: Clive Barda; page 40: Clive Barda;

page 42, centre: Clive Barda; others: The Dance Library (Darryl Williams); page 43: David Buckland.

First published in 1990 by Usborne Publishing Ltd, 83-85 Saffron Hill, London EC1N 8RT, England.

Printed in Spain.   AE 1990.